To Nancy Downs: I hope you enjoy this + get a few chuckles.

Rough Side of the Mountain

D1270540

CARDED

D. Geraldine Lawson

D. Geraldine Lawson

This work is a fictional autobiography. However, in order to give credit and acclaim to those who deserve it, the author retained the real names of mountain storytellers and family members. In addition, local and regional historical events as well as histories of the Robinette, Hall, Bond, McCarty, and Mullins families are accounts and records supplied by local historians and family members. Special thanks go to Hubert Powers of Coeburn and Glen Roberts Jr. of Wise for providing family records.

*Sept. 28, 1996   Michael Clark
Restored Home*

FIRST EDITION

Copyright 1996, by D. Geraldine Lawson
Library of Congress Catalog Card No: 95-90639
ISBN: 1-56002-611-1

UNIVERSITY EDITIONS, Inc.
59 Oak Lane, Spring Valley
Huntington, West Virginia 25704

Cover and interior art by Debbie High

10-4 415

Dedication

This book is dedicated to my Father, James Hall, whose stories and folktales delight the imagination of all who are privileged to know him; and to my Mother, Anna Jean Robinette Hall, for her love, devotion, prayers, and sacrifice on my behalf.

CHAPTER 1

RECOLLECTIONS OF POSSUM HOLLER

"Geraldine, there's a place in the Atlantic Ocean called the Sargasso Sea—a calm place. But it's bad for ships because there's not enough wind for their big sails and they get all tangled up in gulfweed. They can't escape once they're trapped that way . . . so, they stay there till they die." That's the exact words Pansy McCarty said to me when we were both girls of sixteen. I just thought Pansy had been reading books about pirate ships or something so I didn't pay her much attention. I should have listened. But that's not when the story started.

It all started in Wise County, Virginia, way down in Possum Holler, in 1945—the year the big war ended. The big war didn't start or end in Possum Holler mind you, I did. I started there. But I haven't ended anywhere yet.

My parents, James and Anna Jean Hall, covered me with affection during those early years the way frost blankets the meadows on a crisp March morning. And I reckon pleasant childhood memories, like wellsprings, see a person through inevitable droughts and long hot days of summer.

One of the first things I remember is the fair, not the World's Fair, that was in New York or some place. Ours was the Big Fair; and I was so excited that I was up before the roosters, except for this one old red rooster that used to crow at midnight. We allowed he was getting into somebody's corn mash because sometimes he was still staggering when the sun came up. One morning he cocked his head in the air, the way roosters do when they're commencing to crow, and fell clean off the rail fence, backwards. But that's another story.

I had to get ready for the fair because I was entering the flowers I'd made in Sunday School out of pasteboard and pipestem cleaners. But what I really looked forward to was the foot race because I was finally big enough to run in it.

Mother was taking her huckleberry pie from the oven. It looked like Mount Vesuvius, all round and high, with steam shooting out the little fork holes in the top. Daddy couldn't take anything to the fair because he was going to work at the Dunfork coal mine. He had to shoot down some coal for loading Monday morning. Daddy promised me he would get to the fair grounds in time to see me run. He hugged us and struck out across the hill to the coal mine. Mother and I jumped in the Jeep and headed on down Possum Holler. We wound around the little mountain road that was cut off like porch steps, and I closed my eyes and held my breath. My uncle always said that if you ever went off the side of that road, you'd starve to death before you stopped rolling, and I wasn't hankering to starve to death.

The fairgrounds was at an old farm where a little valley and Guest River strolled arm in arm between mountains, like ancient, devoted lovers. We almost had to call it the Happy Valley fair because one of the mountain boys by the name of Fred Greear, went off to school somewhere and became a lawyer. When he came back to the mountains, he bought the old farm and wanted to change the name of the place. Everybody reckoned that Happy Valley would be a real funny name for a place, so it didn't catch on, and we went right on calling it Possum Holler. Still, it was good for a laugh or two.

When we got to the fair, Mother parked the Jeep beside a pick-up truck that had a bunch of barking redbones in the back. A sign on the truck said "straight coon hounds—won't trash—$1 for one—$2 for all." We sure didn't want any more dogs, so we passed it up.

Suddenly the morning air was filled with loud colors and warm spicy steam drifting from the chili and applebutter kettles. Noisy people fluttered and chattered everywhere. It sent goose bumps all over me. When we got half way across the bottom, mother handed me her huckleberry pie, and I struck out lickety split to the judging tables. I was singing "h-a-huckle b-a-buckle h-a-huckle-y, h-a-huckle b-a-buckle, huckleberry pie" as I placed mother's pie between Lizzie Cassell's wild grape jam and Helen Bond's rhubarb marmalade. Then I saw my Uncle Maynard Robinette, mother's brother, walking across the bottom with his molasses cake. He made it from his own fresh cane molasses. It was stacked hot and high. He put it down among some persimmon cookies, a cherry cobbler, and my Grandma Robinette's white chiffon coconut cake made with 13 eggs. Then he looked at me and winked. He knew it was the best on the table.

Across from the food tables were the quilts—the ones made from the new chop sacks. Grandma Robinette (Bessie), entered her double-wedding-ring quilt that year. Grandma made quilts that kings would have been proud to sleep under. But she always just said her quilts put the warm into winter.

The table beside the quilts had what I was looking for—the homemade stuff. A linen handkerchief with a crocheted edge and a blue and yellow butterfly embroidered in one corner caught my eye. I couldn't imagine wiping my nose on something that fancy. Then I recognized a monkey ladder my grandpa, Will Robinette, had made. I looked over all the baskets, pottery, and stringed instruments, then placed my flowers beside a head carved from a stump. I think it was Abraham Lincoln.

About that time, Jim and Jessee McReynolds commenced to play and sing "Lost All My Money But A Two Dollar Bill and I'm On My Long Journey Home." My Grandma Hall was just

6

about the first one to start clogging. She didn't like for you to say she danced because dancing was an abomination to God. She "stepped it off." They kept playing and singing and stepping it off until finally Jim and Jessee started playing "I wonder how the Old Folks are at Home," which got everybody to crying, and then the contests started.

I watched all of the contests from the hog calling to the pole climbing. But the greased pig was my favorite. They got this squealing pig and greased him up real good with lard and turned him loose. Then they hit their britchy legs with their hats and yelled "sooee." The men and boys took out after the pig and the women and children ran after them, laughing and screaming. Of course, the pig ran where he wasn't supposed to be and tore down somebody's quilt before it was over. And there was so much squealing going on, you couldn't tell the pig from the people. Then June Mead caught the pig and held on, so he got to take him home.

Finally it was almost time for the race and I started watching for Daddy. I saw Mother walking toward the road and I knew she was looking for him too. I sat down against the back of the chili stand and chewed the ribbon on the end of my pigtail until I saw him running down the hill toward the fair grounds. He came straight from the coal mine except he had stopped at the honeysuckle holler spring and washed off all the coal dust he could get off. Miners sometimes got coal dust off every spot on their faces except around their eyelids where the lashes grow. It made their eyes look velvety.

I was one of the youngest children in the race that year and all ages could run in it. I'm not making excuses for losing, because I never lost another race in my life. And that particular race I was doing pretty good too until I stepped in something fresh there in the cow pasture and slid and fell. A tall red-haired boy who ran barefoot and had a rag wrapped around his big toe won the race. I just wanted to hide behind a tree and cry.

After the race, however, Mother came up to me smiling and said we'd better check our wares because the judging was over. But Daddy said he'd be heading on across the bottom. When I got close to the craft tables, I saw something shiny on my flowers and sure enough I had won a red ribbon. My grandma's double-wedding-ring quilt won a blue ribbon and Uncle Maynard's cake did too. But for the first time Mother didn't win a ribbon at all. I watched Mother pick up her pie and smile just as big as if she had won a blue ribbon. I decided I'd try to be especially good to her for the next day or so.

We struck out across the bottom and when we got in sight of the jeep, there in the front seat sat Daddy and a big redbone hound, both of them grinning.

As soon as we got home, I washed off, changed clothes, and

ate some chili and slaw and huckleberry pie. Then Mother gave me a book of rhymes she bought at the fair. I tucked it under my arm and started to run straight to Pansy McCarty's house. Mother stopped me and said, "Remember Geraldine, if Mrs. McCarty asks you to eat with them, say 'thank-you just the same, but I've eaten already.' " Mother always reminded me not to eat at Pansy's house because they didn't have food to spare. I assured Mother I wouldn't eat a bite and ran out the door. Pansy was my third cousin and my special friend, but she couldn't walk. She was born that way. I heard a lot of people say that while Pansy's mother was carrying her in the womb, she accidentally laid eyes on a dog that got run over by a coal truck, and that event marked Pansy. But Mother said that's not how things happened. Pansy lived with her mother and grandma in a three-room log house in a little oak grove just past the spring. Pansy's daddy was in the Dunfork coal mine two years earlier when rock and dirt caved in through the roof—that's why she didn't have a daddy.

The McCarty house was steamy hot when I got there because they took in washing and ironing and it was wash day. Pansy's mother carried buckets of water from the spring and heated it in a big pan on the kitchen cookstove. Then she dipped hot water from the pan into a tub on the floor that had a washboard in it. Pansy's grandmother sat at the washboard and scrubbed the clothes, then she wrung them out, and dropped them into the rinse tub. Pansy's mother swished them through the rinse water, wrung them out again and hung them on the clothes line just outside the kitchen door. At our house, Mother had to wash all the clothes and wring them out then empty the wash tub and put rinse water in it because we had only one tub. I always thought it would be awfully nice to have two tubs.

Pansy's mother and grandmother were both short, broad women with long black hair that they kept braided and twisted around on the back of their heads. But on wash day, their braids sagged down their backs and wisps of long hair hung around their faces. Ever so often, they pushed back the hair and sweat with the backs of their hands. I liked the sharp, wet, green-apple smell of wash day, although in the summer it did make it right hot in the house. Of course, all the doors and windows were wide open and a breeze always kept the white lacy curtains fluttering and kept Pansy cooled off a little.

Pansy smiled and laughed a lot and she was an "only child" and I was an "only child" and that made us both special. Sometimes she wore her hair in pigtails like me, but she didn't have the freckles on her nose that I had. Her eyes were round like fifty-cent pieces and dark blue like Guest's River. My eyes were round too but pale blue like the sky near the horizon. And Pansy had a special way of placing her left fist to her temple and patting her head with her index finger. It made her look smarter than a Philadelphia lawyer. I knew when she patted her head that way, she was giving serious thought to everything. Then Pansy usually said, "It seemed like the right thing to do." I told her about the fair and then I told her how I slid and fell. She began to giggle and the first thing you know we both laughed and I didn't feel bad about it anymore. Pansy was that way. I commenced to read my book to her and a wonderful notion popped into my mind. Mother and I could teach Pansy to read from the same books Mother taught me out of. I asked Pansy if she'd like to read like me and she smiled like a possum in a persimmon tree. I thought, however, that when I talked to Pansy about reading, I caught a glimpse of Mrs. McCarty looking sad and shaking her head, but I couldn't tell for sure. She looked sad most of the time anyway. I figured that just because Pansy couldn't go to school didn't mean she shouldn't learn to read books. When Pansy was born they said she wasn't supposed to live but she fooled everybody and lived anyway. Doctor Clement called her a little survivor. Pansy didn't go hardly anywhere, except into the yard a little while on sunny days, because it was hard for her mother and grandmother to carry her much farther than that. So I figured if she could learn to read, the rest wouldn't matter too much.

On the way home I stopped to play in the spring. The water smelled cool and minty because of all the penny royal growing around it. I slipped off my sandals and felt the mud squish between my toes as I dug in the bank of the little stream that ambled off down the mountain. Sometimes, I found arrowheads made from flint rock. I always found rocks—milky smooth ones and sparkly rough ones. I figured one day I'd find gold and we would be rich. Then Daddy wouldn't have to work in the coal mine any longer. I took my little gems home and Mother put down her quilting and helped me clean them and put them in the oatmeal can with the others. I told Mother my idea about teaching Pansy to read and she patted me on the head and said, "Geraldine, you are a little genius."

Daddy was in the kitchen making a collar for his new "no trash" hound dog. I figured that coon hunting helped take his mind off coal mining. He had started working in the Dunfork mine when they re-opened it. I prayed every night that my daddy would always come back to mother and me. But Pansy may have prayed for her Daddy too. I don't know. I started to ask her several times but didn't have the heart.

The Possum Holler Fair was always the week before school started back, so summer was almost over. That meant we couldn't go swimming at the Rock Hole in Guest's River many more times and the church wouldn't have any more picnics on the High Knob after Sunday morning service. And I sure did like swimming and picnicking. To get to the Rock Hole we walked down the tracks of the old Interstate Railroad Line. The hot, sweaty smell of tar and oil and creosote and the roar of that winding river echoing around the rocky bluffs excited the living daylights out of me. I knew every crevice in the rocks and every root to hang on to as we climbed down the cliff that led from the railroad tracks to the river. And I knew exactly how deep to dive when I took the plunge into that dark, slow-moving water from the little rock at the upper end of the hole. And just like everybody else I'd pop up out of the water and yell "whew," and listen to it echo up and up those cliffs, all the way to heaven, I believe. And God knew by our "whews" he had created a good thing when He created the Rock Hole.

Even though our trips to the Rock Hole and the High Knob were about over for another year, we still went to the "Top of the Hill" three or four times a week. We went there for fun all the time. The Top of the Hill was our gathering place. Actually, it was a little one-room general store and a church out the road from it. That's all it was. The store had three more rooms built on to it so the people who owned it would have a place to live. And it seemed that everybody in Possum Holler took turns owning the store and living there; I guess we figured somebody had to do it. Some people called it "The Gap" because it was located in the gap of the mountain at the intersection of the Dry Fork/Crab Orchard road with the Possum Holler road.

Inside the store, there were plenty of cane chairs and kegs scattered around so you could sit down and prop your feet on the old pot-bellied stove and burn your soles off. There was always a big pot of coffee on the stove and nothing smelled any better than coffee grounds boiling and rubber burning at the same time. You had to learn how to pour that kind of coffee. You had to pour it into a cup and back into the pot three or four times to settle the grounds. Otherwise, people complained that their coffee had dregs. Most of the time there were soup beans cooking and corn bread baking on the Warm Morning in the kitchen.

Not long before the fair that year, we put up electric lights outside the store so we could pitch horse shoes after dark. People came from all over Crab Orchard and Dry Fork just to see what it was like to pitch horse shoes under artificial lights. There is a science to pitching horse shoes. You have to learn to pitch the shoe level so it won't roll—get the horse off, we always said. And you make sure that shoe turns one full revolution and lands flat with the open end headed toward the peg, a sidewinder we called it. You usually have learned to pitch by the time the soreness leaves your shoulder and the blister on your thumb hardens.

We kept two checker boards humming year round—most stores had only one. Charles Bond was the champion checker player of all time. Everybody who thought they had got right

10

good at checkers had to take him on. But Uncle Charlie never lost. Beeb Lawson almost won a few times but folks said that was on account of Beeb slipping Uncle Charlie's checkers off the board while he wasn't looking.

Of course, once a year, we had the really big event at the top of the hill—the one that got everyone in Possum Holler all het up. And that was when Sherwin Williams came out with their new colors. I was always the first one there to see it—the color chart that is—not the paint; we had no use for paint. The colors splattered all through my mind. There was no way to express it—not even our best yarn spinners could think of anything to say except, "Well now, would you look at that." I remember my favorite color of all time. Edgewater Blue. I declare I could hear the ocean every time I looked at it. I knew the sound of the ocean; I'd heard it in a big sea shell that my Grandma Robinette kept on the mantle over the fireplace.

Winter always sneaked into the mountains early, and that year was no different. Mother woke me at sun up one soft, fall morning with "Come look. Someone was here last night." I threw back the quilts and splatted barefoot across the cold linoleum rugs. Then I saw them—all shapes and sizes of big, white, sparkly snowflakes on the inside of each window. Mother quietly told me that Jack Frost slipped through the house while we slept and cast his tears on all our panes.

I was glad cold weather was upon us because I liked winter best at the Top of the Hill. On week-ends and when school was closed we rode sleighs all day long. We had one real curvy three mile run to Dry fork, but that was a long walk back except when we could get my daddy to pull us back with a rope tied to his Jeep. Our other favorite run was down Churchhouse Hill. That was where Possum Holler road went down the hill past the church house. It was nearly a mile straight down.

There were about ten of us kids that rode that winter, and we raced down that mountain like maniacs and hardly ever wrecked except for one time, and it was our fault then. Several of us got there early and made one trip down the mountain and got to talking on the way back about how much fun it would be if we could play a trick on the others. So we built a big snow bank about half way down the run and hid and watched for the others to come down. Well, Frank Mays was the first one down and when he hit the snow bank something went wrong and he didn't come out the other end like he was supposed to. He came out the side and went through the barbed wire fence and over the edge of the mountain. We figured him for dead. We climbed down the mountain to look for him and I knew in my heart that when my mother found out I'd killed somebody she would kill me. We found his sleigh first; then we saw a clump of clothes beside an old black walnut tree. But some of the boys hollered

11

back that he was alive and they began to drag him out from under the mountain. We took him to my house because my mother always wanted to be a nurse—and she dressed him up and dressed us down and we never did anything that stupid again, at least not for a while.

After we rode sleighs all day and got cold and wet and happy, we went into the store and got some hot chocolate—the older kids could drink coffee. Then we pulled cane chairs up and stuck our shoes on the stove and listened to the sizzle and watched the steam come off until it finally turned to smoke. Warm and satisfied, we rode back down Churchhouse Hill and home. After the miners got home, we all went back up to the Top of the Hill store to listen to stories told by the Possum Holler yarn spinners. They were no doubt the best stories to cross the human tongue since God confused the language at the tower of Babel.

On one particular night, my daddy commenced to tell the stories as everyone prepared to listen. I reached down into the pop cooler and grabbed a Grapette out of the ice. Grapettes always formed little ice crystals inside the bottles as soon as you opened them. But I saw it was still snowing outside so I put the Grapette back and got another cup of hot chocolate instead. Then I got a moon pie and tried to lean my chair back on its back two legs while I propped my feet on the stove. I pushed back a little too far and turned the chair over. That gave everybody a good laugh even before the stories started. So I just sat up straight and stuck my shoes against the stove. It wasn't comfortable but it was the way you had to sit when you listened to stories at the Top of the Hill. I was ready.

Daddy started off with his "Uncle Dan Ramey" stories. Uncle Dan had lived in the early 1900's and at that time there was such a love for the whopper that Wise County, where we lived, held an annual liar's contest. "Well," Daddy began, "Uncle Dan had won the liar's contest every year, hands down. So it was right unusual one year when he didn't show up on time with his lie. Just as the contest was getting underway, somebody saw him coming a-running. Dan poked his head into where they was all gathered and told them he didn't come for no contest, he was in a rush. 'Why what in the world you in such a hurry for,' somebody asked him. 'Begod'—Begod was his word—'I gotta git on over to the funeral parlor,' Uncle Dan said, all out of breath. 'Dice'—Dice was his wife—'Dice, she died deddern hell last night.' Well Dan, he hurried on and the liar's convention kind of broke up as everyone was all tore up over Dice being dead and all. In a minute here come Dan a-sneaking in the back way a-grinning. He just looked at everyone and said, 'Well, begod, that's my lie, now what do you have to say for yourselves?' Course Uncle Dan, he won again."

Everybody liked Uncle Dan stories. Uncle Victor, Daddy's brother, asked if Uncle Dan wasn't involved in politics right much. Daddy said Uncle Dan never did run for public office himself, but he campaigned for whoever was running on the democrat ticket. So Uncle Dan always went down to the polls and stood and gave speeches and beat his hat against the podium until he wore it out. Every year the democrats bought him a new hat. We laughed and laughed about that because almost everybody in the county was democrats. I took another bite of my moon pie and a big sworp of hot chocolate and settled back for more. I could smell the rubber soles burning and I knew everybody was real happy. I looked over at Lucy Smith and Shirley Davis, my two good friends, and they looked at me and somehow we knew, we just knew in our hearts, it would never be better than this. The stories about the democrats just kept coming until Uncle Maynard finally told the story I was waiting to hear. Uncle Maynard said he was told that the democrats, along about Uncle Dan's time, had a habit of voting the cemetery every year. One year, as two of the better known politicians, a couple of the Bond brothers, were visiting a particular cemetery to collect names to vote, they ran upon a tomb stone with the name Su Lang Wu. "Wait a minute," one of them said, "we can't vote him, he's a foreigner." After considerable thought the other one replied, "He's got as good a right to vote as anybody in this here cemetery." And since that was a true statement they voted Mr. Wu also.

After everybody stopped laughing, June Mead asked why in tarnation the democrats wanted to vote the cemetery when purt near every voter was a democrat anyway. Allen Hale said he reckoned that the democrats figured that you just couldn't be too careful.

The story about a cemetery got them started telling stories about mountain people living to be real old. Each one knew somebody that lived to be older than the last one until Bob Davis finally said that he was squirrel hunting way back up toward the High Knob one time when he run upon a real old man sitting on a rock, crying. Down in the holler below was a little sawmill style house with smoke coming out the chimney and a bunch of crying babies and barking dogs. He figured the old codger lived down there and he might have to help him get back. Bob said the man was so old that two wrinkles was all that was left of his face, and he was chewing tobacco with them. So Bob decided to ask him why he was crying. "Paw whooped me," came the reply. Bob was so startled that he near took leave of his senses, he said, but he managed to ask why his paw whooped him. "Because I hit Grandpa with a rock as he was working in the garden," the old man explained as he continued to sob.

That story topped the evening off real well. We somehow

knew when the best story had been told. Or maybe we knew it was time to quit when the smell of burning rubber was strong enough. Anyway, we got on our coats and headed home. Most everybody lived down in Possum Holler. When my mother and daddy and I got to our little brown wooden house, I headed straight for bed. I could make out the sounds of ashes being shoveled into a bucket and the Warm Morning being banked with coal for the night. The railroad engineer gave two long tugs on the whistle as the old coal train rolled down Guest's River. Daddy closed the front door, and I closed my eyes for sleep. No one in Possum Holler ever locked their houses.

CHAPTER 2

FETCH LIGHTS AND FUNERALS

Pansy's reading lessons came along real well that first winter. Mother took my chalkboard and books over to her house. Then every evening after school, Mother met me there and we taught her all the letters of the alphabet and the sounds they make. It wasn't long before Pansy could figure out new words just by looking at them and pronouncing all the sounds. She put her little fist beside her temple and pecked the words right into her head with her finger. One day I wrote "hippopotamus" on the chalkboard and Pansy said it out loud on the first try. We laughed and giggled over that until Mother made me leave the room. By Christmas, Pansy could read the "Fun with Dick and Jane" and the "Friends and Neighbors" books. And by the time school was out that summer she could read anything we could find to take to her. She could even read the Bible. Pansy's grandmother had taken an interest in her reading and taught her to read the King James Bible because she thought every child should learn to read God's word.

The Dry Fork school teacher heard about Pansy and started taking library books to her to read. She visited her several times that summer. She also taught Pansy to write her letters and numbers and to work some arithmetic. The teacher didn't have to do it either, she just wanted to. Pansy was becoming the most educated kid in Possum Holler.

Spring and summer kept most people busy with gardening and canning. And every spring, Grandma told Daddy that she planted her potatoes in the dark of the moon, and every spring, Daddy told Grandma he preferred to plant his in the ground. And that exchange always kicked off our planting season. Anyway, it was a busy summer for me too because that spring Mother and Daddy gave me my own little garden plot. Daddy plowed and harrowed it for me, but I got to plant the seeds and fertilize and water them. After the planting, I watched every day for them to peep up out of the ground. Finally the heads of little plants were smiling and nodding at me from every direction. I stood in the middle of it all and wondered at the new creation brought forth by my own hands. I figured it must have been a little like God felt a long time ago.

Then Mother told me that my peas had to be thinned. She said they were coming up too thick so I must pinch off the littlest ones and the bent ones and discard them. But I didn't do it. It's not that I didn't try; but when you've planted the little seeds in the ground and watched them wiggle up through the earth and reach for life, you can't just throw them away. Every day my peas got paler and skinnier. I looked at Daddy's and Mother's garden. Their garden had neat little rows of healthy, green plants one and one-half feet apart. I decided I would try giving my plants extra water and fertilizer. But finally one day Mother told me that I couldn't go back over to Pansy's house anymore until I thinned the peas in my garden. So I pinched off the little plants and threw them out of the garden because I really wanted to see Pansy. I understood something right then and there; little peas don't have a chance in this world.

One day after I had been over to Pansy's to see the new books the school teacher brought her, I spotted Daddy's Jeep just as I rounded the bend from the spring. It was parked in its usual place by the road in front of the house even though Daddy wasn't supposed to be home until later. I ran home as fast as I could but then I stopped at the door. I was afraid. I wanted to run back to Pansy's house. I wanted to run to my grandma's. I didn't want to hear what I was afraid I might hear. I didn't want anything to change. I slipped into the front room but no one was there. I stood real still and listened.

Then I heard voices in the kitchen. I could hear Mother talking in a strange way. I almost started to cry. Then I heard his voice too. The most beautiful voice on the earth—the voice of my daddy. I ran to the kitchen. Mother was crying and Daddy was saying something, I couldn't tell what. I cried too. Mother sat down at the kitchen table and picked me up. She started rocking back and forth and telling me not to worry, everything would be all right. Then they told me what had happened. The miners had come on the outside to eat lunch. But Buddy McCoy had gone back into the mine to make sure he had turned off a motor. While he was inside, the roof caved in. Daddy was taking some more tools back to help see if they could dig through the rock and coal and find him. They found him the next day; he was dead.

The families of miners always cry and go on so at funerals. And mothers, especially, cry and hold onto the casket and have to be pulled away. They held Buddy's funeral at the church at the Top of the Hill. Buddy was the youngest of the McCoy brothers, just eighteen. He rode sleighs with us down that same hill last winter. His mother was white-headed so I figured she was right old. Buddy's daddy was sitting right beside her. He kept lifting that rough, wrinkled hand and rubbing it down the side of his face to wipe away the tears. It just didn't seem right for old people to have to live with that kind of hurt. The preacher at our church there at the Top of the Hill was Charles Ruff. And everybody always said he could preach the prettiest funeral sermons they ever heard. People said that when he preached, you would just as soon trade places with the dead person in the casket because he made heaven sound so good. I listened real close but I didn't want to trade.

The church was actually Mt. Olivette Presbyterian Church. The mountains were settled mainly by Scotch-Irish, so the Presbyterians felt obliged to send missionaries into the mountains and establish churches because that was our heritage. We learned all about it in Sunday School. They said that in the early 1920's, Mary Martin was sent to Wise county as a missionary from Staunton, Virginia. She established four Presbyterian churches in the mountains. Daddy said that when Mary Martin came to Mt. Olivette Church, she brought a speaker one Sunday morning that she called doctor somebody or other—Daddy couldn't remember the name. No one there had ever heard anyone except a medical doctor called "doctor." So when church let out, instead of telling him what a good sermon he preached, they commenced to tell him about their aches, pains, and ills.

Times were hard back then and the mountain folk couldn't afford lumber to build churches. So Mt. Olivette Church at the Top of the Hill and Bethany church on Dry Fork and the Pine Chapel on Bull Run were all built out of old wood taken from churches in the deserted mining towns. Mt. Olivette was built with lumber from a church that had been abandoned at Little Toms Creek. The church building at Virginia City was already there because Virginia City had once been a booming mining community and the mining company had built the church. The church was closed when the mining boom ended, but when Mary Martin came, she started it back up as a Presbyterian Church.

Daddy told me that the children pulled nails out of boards from the abandoned churches and saved them to re-use because the people couldn't even afford nails. He remembered because he pulled and straightened hundreds of nails himself. He was just about nine years old at the time. There was already a Presbyterian Church established at Coeburn. So all five churches became known as the Mary Martin Memorial. Dick Pate was the one who suggested the name.

Before Mt. Olivette Presbyterian church was established, there was a church in Crab Orchard called Methodist Protestant Church. By the time I was born it was called Bond Memorial Methodist Church. A lot of Bonds lived in Crab Orchard and Uncle Nathan Bond was a big worker in the church so that's how it got its name. Although, Daddy said, it was Uncle Bob Buchanan that did most of the manual labor when the church was built. The story I liked best about Bond Memorial Church was that my great grandmother, Catherine McCarty, was once the pastor of it. They said that Ma—most everybody called her Aunt Catherine but the family called her Ma—could pray heaven down. When somebody in the mountains took sick, they called for Ma and then the doctor and always in that order because Ma got there first and did a lot more good. Ma had died just a few months earlier and Mother and Daddy took me to her wake. I sat all night and watched her lying in her casket in the living room of my great aunt Norma Buchanan's house. Several times I saw her chest move up and down so I figured she must still be alive. But I don't guess she was because they buried her the next day. I remembered how Ma used to sit by the fire and smoke her pipe and plait her long black hair. She could whittle good, and she took her knife and found little animals in pieces of wood for me. She told me that when she was a little girl like me, life was a lot simpler. She said there were only two things you had to remember. One was, always whittle away from yourself, and the other was, never eat yellow snow. That was all.

The oldest church still standing when I was born was one on Dry Fork. It was Cherry Grove Free Will Baptist Church. There were more Free Will Baptist Churches in the mountains, at that time, than any other churches. I don't know how that happened except that the Free Will Baptists preached loud and beat on the pulpit and talked about hell fire and sin, and the mountain folk were partial to rousing speeches. But you'd hear most people say that it didn't make no never mind which church they went to, so everybody just went to the churches in their own hollers and hills. That's why all of us in Possum Holler went to the church at the Top of the Hill. And that's why that every time somebody from Possum Holler got killed in a coal mine they had the funeral there.

I didn't get to go to Buddy's wake. Mother and Daddy didn't want me staying up all night so I stayed at Grandpa Robinette's house. But I was glad to get to go to the funeral. Buddy's funeral was not much different from all the other funerals. My mother and daddy and Beeb Lawson and Claude Hays sang three quartet songs. They were called the Mount Olivette Quartette and singing at funerals and revival meetings was their specialty. They sang all around, even over in Kentucky. All of their funeral songs were slow and mournful sounding—sung in minor music. Mother and Daddy stood in front with Claude and Beeb behind, peering over their shoulders at the songbook. Daddy keyed up on the pitchpipe and they sang "We are Going Down the Valley One by One" and "Where the Shades of Love Lie Deep."[1]

We are often bowed with a load of sorrow
When our loved ones fall asleep

1. Where The Shades Of Love Lie Deep, O.A. Parris & Eugene Wright (C) Copyright 1931 (renewal 1959) Tennessee Music and Printing/ASCAP a div. of Pathway Music, P.O. Box 2250, Cleveland, TN 37320 in Radiant Gems. Used by permission.

> *But we'll meet again on some glad tomorrow*
> *Where the shades of love lie deep*

Then Mr. Ruff preached his sermon and ended it by raising one arm high over his head and asking God's grace on everyone. I always liked that prayer. It made me feel safe. After that, the quartet sang "Gloryland"[2] just before everyone filed around by the casket for one last look at Buddy. The last verse went:

> *But fear not friends, I'm going home*
> *Up there to die no more*
> *No coffins will be made up there*
> *No graves on that fair shore.*

It was right comforting thought.

After the funeral they buried Buddy in the Bond graveyard on the mountain above my house. The road went straight up the side of the hill. I never could understand why graveyards were always on the very top. I guess it was either because they had to find a level spot or because it was closer to heaven. Anyway, that was the first time I got to help carry flowers. My grandpa, Oscar Hall, had dug the grave. About every time somebody died, he dug the grave. But a lot of men brought shovels and helped cover Buddy. We placed flowers all over the grave and still had flowers left over, so Buddy's mother said to put them on other graves. I put some colorful bunches on Pansy's daddy's grave and on Ma's grave. Finally, everybody gathered around the grave on the top of that mountain, and the men removed their hats. Then in the stillness we sang:

> *What a friend we have in Jesus*
> *All our sins and griefs to bear*
> *What a privilege to carry*
> *Everything to God in prayer.*
>
> *Have we trials and temptations*
> *Is there trouble anywhere*
> *We should never be discouraged*
> *Take it to the Lord in prayer.*

It was Buddy's favorite song. There was something, though, that I didn't understand about all of it. I figured one day I would. Before we left the hill, relatives visited loved ones' graves and pointed out where they wanted to be buried when they died. "Now when I die," Grandma said, "I want to be layed beside

---

2. Reprinted by permission of the publisher, Hopper Brothers and Connie Publishing.

Ma, and I want Oscar to be put right here beside me." She said it matter-of-factly just like when she told Grandpa, "Now I want my red rosebush here between the boxwood and George Washington's bridal wreath."

My family didn't go to Buddy's house after the funeral, we went home. Mother had already taken a big pot of chicken and dumplings, a pan of ham biscuits, a heaping bowl of cressy greens, and a three-layer chocolate cake down to the McCoy house the day of the wake. And anyway, when we got back home, Mother started cooking supper for us and talking to Daddy about leaving the coal mine. She told him she just couldn't bear the thought of his going back to the mine again. Daddy didn't much want to quit because coal mines had started paying a little better wages the last few years. But Daddy saw that Mother and I were awful troubled about it, and he wasn't going to get shed of us until he gave in. So Daddy said he would buy a coal truck and haul coal for a living. He was worried about making enough money for us though; I could tell. It took two people to haul coal and most of the time two men would go in together and buy the truck. Then they split the money they made. But Mother told Daddy she would ride with him and it would help make more money. After Daddy agreed to hauling coal for a living, we sat down and asked God's blessings on us and thanked him for the soup beans and dumplings, greens, pickled beets, corn bread, and butter milk. I don't ever remember eating so much.

After supper, Mother and Daddy fed the animals and I went out in the front yard to swing. But the sun was setting behind the grave yard and long finger-like shadows crept closer and closer to our little house. I asked Mother and Daddy if we could walk out to Grandma Hall's and sit a spell and they said okay and we headed out the road. Grandma and Grandpa had just got back from the McCoy house and they said you never saw such a crowd or so much food in your life. Grandma went into the back room and came out with her big, black family Bible she kept in the trunk. She wrote Buddy's name and date of death in the front under "obituaries" where she kept a record of everybody's deaths, whether they were family or not. It was her Mother's (Ma McCarty) Bible and Ma had recorded births and deaths in it until she died. Every now and then, Grandma would get the Bible out and show me people's names under "births" and, a few pages over, the same names under "obituaries." It made life seem like it was just a few pages long—you're born, you turn a few tattered pages, and you're dead.

After she recorded his name, Grandma told us that Buddy's Aunt said she knew Buddy's death was a-comin because she had seen a fetch light at his window just the night before. By the time Grandma told us about the fetch light, it was dark outside and as I looked out the window I could see three lights on the ridge above Pansy's house. It scared me until I heard Grandma's rooster crow and then I knew it was just some possum hunters. Whenever possum hunters crossed the ridge with their carbide lights on their heads, Grandma's old red rooster would crow. Still, I moved over to the big chair in the corner behind the stove. Then I got comfortable and sleepy. As I dozed off I dimly remember hearing talk about Lizzy Cassell's neuralgia acting up on her again and the phone lines getting closer to Possum Holler. Daddy must have carried me home—I woke up in my bed the next morning.

The next Sunday at the end of the church service we gathered in a circle and held hands. Then we dismissed with a song that helped me feel a little better about the happenings of the last few days:

Tempted and Tried we're oft made to wonder
Why it should be thus all the day long
While there are others living about us
Never molested though in the wrong.

Chorus
Farther along we'll know all about it
Father along we'll understand why
Cheer up my brother, live in the sunshine
We'll understand it all by and by.[3]

That Monday, Daddy bought a coal truck and two shovels: one for him and one for Mother.

3. Farther Along, J.R. Baxter, Jr. and W. B. Stevens (C) Copyright 1937 Stamps-Baxter Music/BMI. All Rights Reserved. Used by permission of Benson Music Group, Inc.

CHAPTER 3

MOTHER'S HANDS

I liked this coal-hauling business a lot because I got to help. Daddy took the truck down to Dry Fork to a coal mine around on the side of a mountain and backed it up to the tipple. He loaded up with five to six tons of coal. Daddy always got small lumps of coal. They called the small sizes "egg" and "nut." Daddy stood on the sideboards of the truck and lowered a long wooden pole which raised a trap door and let the coal pour down the chute and into the truck bed. Daddy watched the coal for any rock and slate. If he saw either, he picked it out and threw it away. After the front half of the truck bed was loaded, Daddy pulled the truck up and loaded the back half. Then he stood on the coal in the front of the truck to watch for more rock and slate. While he loaded the truck, he let me play on the near-by slate dump and look for fossils. Daddy told me all about slate being full of pictures of little animals and fern-like leaves that lived a long time ago. I thought it was right smart of God to press those little memories into the slate and store them under mountains until the coal miners came along and dug them out for everybody to see.

Early the next morning, before I woke up, Mother carried me to the truck and we headed out toward Abingdon. After I woke up Mother gave me breakfast, a fried egg sandwich and a cup of milk. Nothing tastes better when you are riding up the road along about Buzzard's Roost in a coal truck. We sold coal all the way from Abingdon to Roanoke. We got about ten dollars a ton. We had to pay three to four dollars a ton, depending on the grade. The farther we had to haul the coal before we sold it, the less we made on a load, Daddy said. The farthest we ever hauled a load of coal was right on top of Bent Mountain, at Roanoke. The people at Bent Mountain had a little girl my age. She had a ponytail and she liked to shake her head and make it hit her face. She wore shorts and had a store bought swing set. We didn't talk much except she told me her name was Dorothy and I told her my name was Geraldine. Then we played on her swing set while Mother and Daddy unloaded coal for the people. Mother threw a shovel full of coal for every one that Daddy threw.

People owned coal stoves and coal furnaces and they needed the coal to cook and keep warm. So it wasn't too hard to sell a load of coal. We just stopped at houses and asked the people if they'd be needing any coal. Daddy still didn't like hauling coal, no more money than he was making. We didn't get to sell but two and sometimes three loads a week. But Daddy wasn't inside the coal mine and that's what mattered. I prayed every night that he would never have to go back under the mountain.

My Grandpa Robinette still worked in the coal mine. He had a bad heart and bad lungs and sometimes the air in the mine wasn't too good. I remember Grandpa saying that death by the name of Chokedamp prowled those tunnels, blowing out carbide lamps. So when Grandpa got out of the mine in the evening he had to stretch out beside the road several times on his way home before he could walk any farther. My Grandma worried so much about him when he was a little later than usual getting home that she stood by the road, summer or winter, and asked the other miners as they came by if they had seen him. "Bessie, I saw Will about a half mile down the road a-resting. So he'll be along directly." That's what they usually said. But I never once heard Grandpa complain. He just did his job and had nothing but a kind word for everybody. I prayed for Grandpa every night too.

One evening when we got back from selling a load of coal, Frank Mays came to the house and told us that his brothers from Baltimore were in for a visit and asked us to come down for some singing and playing. After supper we drove to their house way on down in Possum Holler. They lived on the side of the hill not far from Guest's River. When we got there, they were already tuned up and we could hear them playing "Ashes of Love." We went inside and the first thing I noticed was the most elegant woman I'd ever laid eyes on. Frank's brother, Jerry, had married a Baltimore woman. She had hair as black as coal and it was fixed around her head with little curls in all the right places. Her shiny-red lips were as red as pokeberries, and her skin was as smooth as a newborn pig's. But I couldn't take my eyes off her hands. I had never seen hands like that on a grown-up. They looked like milk after the cream is churned off. There were no wrinkles, not even at the knuckles. Instead, each knuckle had one little dimple in the center of it. And on her finger was a ring that shined even more than the rocks I found at the spring. She was a wonder of creation. All of a sudden, Mother's hands caught my eye. Then I knew what made the difference. My mother's hands showed a lot of toil. Mother scrubbed our clothes on a wash board every week. She put bleach in the water to clean everything. She hoed the garden and worked in the fields and helped make molasses and canned hundreds of jars of food every summer. She sewed or crocheted or quilted almost everything we owned. And now that she was shoveling coal too, her hands were looking rugged as raspberries. But what bothered me was that my mother's hands didn't have the pleasure of beautiful rings. If any hands in the world deserved big shiny rings, my mother's hands did. I decided right then and there that I would buy my mother a beautiful ring to wear on one of her fingers. After a lot of playing and singing, Mother said we'd better be getting on back home, and as we went out of hearing

23

we could still hear them going strong. The last song I heard was "Wildwood Flower."

The next morning right after my favorite breakfast of tomato gravy and biscuits, I hurried toward Grandma Hall's house to take a looksee at her Sears-Roebuck catalog. I wound my way through the lifeless fog that had settled into the hollers, and filled my lungs with the harsh smell of coal smoke from stoves that had just been stoked for breakfast. When I got to the back porch of Grandma's house, coffee and biscuits drowned out the smell of coal smoke, and through the screen door, I saw Grandma putting squirrel and squirrel gravy on the table. So I ate breakfast again before I started looking in the catalog. I told Grandma I was hankering for a pair of roller skates. I didn't want anyone to know about the ring. There were three pages of rings that had Fine, Finer, and Finest qualities of diamonds. The catalog said the Fine quality rings were not as perfect as Finer, but were still radiantly beautiful and equal to the best quality sold by many stores. The finer quality had no flaws visible to the naked eye; and the Finest was perfect, meaning it had no flaws when magnified 10 times. I finally decided on a Finer quality ring with "gracefully twining garland of white gold orange blossoms on the 14K yellow gold." I had never seen a more beautiful ring. The one-fourth carat diamond, which looked plenty big in its "magic reflector setting," would run me $119.95. I had saved almost five dollars, because, for the last couple of years, Grandma Robinette and Mother had paid me to help them wash canning jars. I got a nickel for each jar I washed. Of course, at these prices, I figured I'd have to wash several thousand more jars before I could send away for the ring. I allowed, however, that I could dig ginseng and sell any scrap metal I found and it wouldn't take so long to get the money. I could feel my heart pounding because I knew for a fact that Mother would one day have that ring.

The next Saturday was absolutely the hottest day of the year. It wasn't supposed to be that hot because summer was almost over. Anyway, just after Mother finished her milking and churning, we saw Martha Lawson scurrying out the road. We were afraid that Martha's husband, Labourn, had took sick, but Martha said she had just heard about a meeting and wanted to know if Mother would take her to it. Martha was a good woman and went to church at the Top of the Hill a lot, but she also went to snake handling meetings every time they held one in the area. Daddy was already helping my grandpa rob his bees, so Mother loaded me and Martha up in the coal truck and we headed for the meeting up between Norton and Wise. The snake handlers were gathered over in a big field and when we got there we could hear them singing and playing guitars. Martha jumped out of the truck and said she wouldn't be long. Mother parked the truck and opened the doors to give us a little more air. The snake handlers were under the only shade tree in the field so we were parked out under the hot, boiling-down sun. Although I told Mother several times I was suffocating to death, she wasn't about to let me out of the truck because she was afraid one of the big rattlers would get away and crawl off through the grass and weeds and I would step on it and get bit and die. By that time, I wasn't sure which death would be worse. And besides that, from our vantage point in the coal truck, I could see children running around down there playing with the snakes just like everyone else. Something about the whole thing didn't make any sense to me. After a lot of singing and playing music and shouting, Martha came back to the truck with the "touch of God on her." Mother inquired of Martha about the people lying on the ground but Martha said they weren't bit, they were just "overcome with the Spirit." We pulled out of there and I heard Mother breathe a sigh of relief as she double-clutched that big coal truck on back toward Possum Holler. Martha thanked us considerable when we got home. Mother and I sat down in the porch swing, plum tuckered out, and Martha went back out the road singing "Victory in Jesus." Then Mother explained to me that some people's religious practices may seem a bit peculiar, but that we feel they're entitled to their own beliefs. About that time, Daddy came back from working in Grandpa's bees. He'd been stung three times.

CHAPTER 4

STONE FOUNDATIONS

That winter started out like any other winter. I visited Pansy every day on my way home from school. Then all of us kids rode sleighs until dinner. After dinner we went back up to the Top of the Hill. But suddenly, everybody in school started getting sore throats. When somebody in school came down with something, everybody got it. I guess it was because of our drinking water. That's what Mother said. We took turns carrying two buckets of water from the spring in the holler every morning when school opened up. We liked to do it because we got out of class. Two of us carried one bucketful each. We kept the water in the cloakroom with a dipper hanging on the wall over it.

After recesses and lunch every day, we filed into the cloakroom for a drink of water. Most of us folded sheets of paper into drinking cups—a drinking cup fold is similar to a sailor's hat fold but nothing like an airplane fold. But some of the kids didn't want to waste a sheet of paper on a cup so they drank straight from the dipper. Then the whole school came down with sore throats. But my sore throat turned into tonsillitis. Dr. Rivers kept giving me penicillin but my tonsils stayed swollen.

One day when Mother took me to see Dr. Rivers, he listened to my heart. He sent me straight to Dr. Short in Norton and he diagnosed it as rheumatic fever. He scheduled me for surgery to get my tonsils removed. It scared me a little because everybody said I was going to get my tonsils pulled. That sounded like it might cause some misery. But Dr. Short told me I wouldn't feel a thing because I would be asleep. He was right. It wasn't bad at all because when I got back home my grandparents brought yip sticks and monkey ladders for me to play with and everybody brought ice cream for me to eat.

I was supposed to get plenty of rest that winter because of the rheumatic fever so I did a lot of my school work at home. And when we went some place, Mother and Daddy wrapped a quilt around me, head and ears, and carried me to the Jeep. One winter's evening I was a Pansy's house while all the other kids rode sleighs. I had just never thought what that was like before. I thought about it then. And as I looked at Pansy I couldn't hardly keep from crying, but she was laughing and telling me about something she had read in one of the books the school teacher gave her. Then we started talking about winter and she told me that winter was a gone-green color, the color of silence and the sound of darkness, deep darkness. "And it's a time when bold trees bow on mummy knees," she said. I never heard anything so beautiful, especially from someone who never got out in winter except at Christmas. But Pansy had a real way with words.

My health improved a little by summer but I still couldn't go swimming at the rock hole in Guest's river. Besides the Top of the Hill store and church, the rock hole was my favorite place in all the world. After church, most all the families packed a picnic and headed for the river. But that summer, we went home. It worked out for the best, though, because I spent more time at my grandma Robinette's and grandma Hall's houses than I ever had before. That's because Mother and Daddy were still hauling coal. Two or three times a week they let me stay with one of my grandmas while they took off a load of coal. Usually they got back in time to take me home at night, but I spent the night with Grandma and Grandpa if they got back right late. Daddy searched the slate piles every time he loaded the truck and brought the little fossils to me. One day he brought a piece of slate that had a black, shiny fern all the way up one side. One of the leaves looked like it had a tiny butterfly perched on the tip of it. I wrapped up that piece of slate in a handkerchief before I put it away.

My grandparents spoiled me on account of me being sick. When I stayed with them, I got ice cream any time I cleared my throat and complained a little. It actually made the whole thing worth while.

There were always a lot of people at Grandma Robinette's house. Grandma's Daddy, John Mullins, and Grandma's brother, Delmer Mullins lived with them. Mother's sister, Mary, who was courting age, was still home too. Grandma was Grandpa's second wife. His first wife was Ida Hall, the daughter of Johnny Hall and Johnny's first wife. Ida died of stomach trouble. When Grandma and Grandpa married, Grandpa had two beautiful little girls, Elsie and Beulah, ages seven and nine, who Grandma took to raise as her own. Then Grandma and Grandpa had six more children. So, during the summer, there were always a lot of family visiting at Grandma's house, making it an exciting place to be. And every summer, my uncle Ralph Robinette's daughter, Diana, came in from Norfolk to spend the summer. That's why I liked to stay at my Grandma Robinette's house.

Diana was just a year younger than me and we liked to do the same things—like gathering eggs from the henhouse. But Grandma had some hens that were laying out. So she paid us a nickel for each nest we found.

We were double trouble for Delmer and Mary. Once we made Delmer keep smoking his cigarettes, one right after another, until he got sick and dizzy. He swore off cigarettes forever. But a week later he was rolling them again. We mostly teased Mary about her boyfriends. Grandpa had run a wire from the house to a tree beside the road where they parked their cars.

27

He hooked up a light on the tree. When Mary came in from her dates, Diana and I flipped the light switch on and off to make them think they were being signaled by Grandma. And one time, when Mary's boyfriend, Carl Morgan, came calling, Grandma paid us a nickel each to call him Uncle Carl. He was a tall, slim man. And when Diana and I called him Uncle Carl, he turned pale and wilted like a wildflower in sunshine.

Mary worked at the sewing factory in St. Paul so she had money to buy cosmetics for herself. Diana and I helped ourselves to her perfume and make-up and nail polish—always with Grandma's blessing. Diana loved animals and rocks. I figured that was because both were in short supply in Norfolk. Once, when we were gathering rocks for Diana to take back to Norfolk, she dropped a heavy one on Mary's foot and broke her big toe. But we took real good care of Mary while she was laid up. We told jokes and imitated different people to make her laugh. We got her laughing so hard one night at the supper table that she got choked on a piece of chicken and turned blue before Grandma finally got that hunk of meat dislodged. Grandpa was praying and Delmer was crying before it was over and Diana and I were scared to death. We thought we had done Mary in for good that time.

While I was sick and couldn't get out much, Daddy got me a pet crow and a pet squirrel and two pet coons. Diana got those animals to enjoying riding the Jeep with me. We started taking them to Pansy's house when we visited her and she loved them as much as Diana did. The squirrel, Otto, and the coons, Mutt and Jeff, would cling to Pansy when we started to leave. The crow, Blackjack, didn't care. Crows don't care about anything much except pestering and pilfering. It wasn't long before Otto and Mutt and Jeff stayed at Pansy's house as much as they did mine. Pansy enjoyed the animals so much that I didn't mind giving them up part of the time.

What Diana and I loved best were the stories. Grandpa lit an oil lamp at night and sat down between it and the wall. He put his hands together to throw shadows on the wall that looked like animals and all sorts of creatures. Then he told stories by having the animals talk to each other—just the way he did for his children when they were little and the way his daddy and grandpa did for their children.

Grandpa told us a lot about his mother and daddy and what it was like when he was growing up. Grandpa's daddy, Henry Robinette, was the son of Mathias and Annie Robinette. Annie's parents were Daniel and Lucinda Hall. The Robinettes were French and Annie's mother was Irish. Henry Robinette's wife was Mary Holbrook, daughter of James and Fannie Holbrook. Henry grew flax and Mary spun the fibers into linen thread. Then she made linen clothes for all the family and curtains and tablecloths and everything they needed for the house. Henry drove a wagon to Abingdon and picked up goods, brought them back, and pedaled them from house to house. Before the railroad was built, that was the only way to get household items and farming tools and salt and sugar to mountain people. The trip took more than two days by wagon. Mary even made a linen cover for Henry's wagon. They saved the flax seed for cooking oil and for lighting their lamps and also for planting another crop. Besides their crops, they raised sheep, cows, chickens, and hogs; and always had a team of mules or oxen. Grandpa said mountain people were right self-sufficient back then before the coal industry moved in. There was a saying that you give an Irishman ten acres of hillside land and he could support a wife and half-a-dozen children on it. There were plenty of big trees in the mountains so a lot of men made a living getting out timber. Some men trapped because there was lots of game in the mountains as well. Others made a decent living from apple orchards, and mountains grew the best apples in the country. The old mountain people knew how to take care of their own and help a neighbor when there was a need.

Religion had come to be real important by the time Grandpa was growing up and he told us that most of his family were Hard Shell Baptists. There were a lot of Hard Shell and Soft Shell Baptists in the mountains when he was a little boy. The Hard Shells didn't believe in a hell that burned for ever and ever, but the Soft Shells did. Otherwise, they were about the same. Some of Grandpa's uncles were Hard Shell preachers. Grandpa said they didn't hold a lot of meetings because they believed that God would save whoever He chose to save anyhow. They believed in living a strict Christian life and being as good as you could be to everyone and praying and reading the Bible and hoping that you were one of the chosen. They didn't believe in musical instruments or songbooks in their churches either. So when they commenced to sing, the preacher "lined" the song. That meant he recited a verse then the whole congregation sang it; then he recited the next verse and so on until they had sung the whole song that way.

Grandpa said one Sunday morning they were about to sing Amazing Grace when a dog wandered into the church. The preacher looked at the congregation and said, "Put out the dog and shut the door," to which the congregation replied "put out the dog and shut the door," to the tune of Amazing Grace.

Grandpa told us about a funeral his parents took him to when he was young. He said that a middle-aged man, stooped real bad with rheumatism, uped and died. And in order to get the man in his casket they had to tie him down with a cord. The Hard Shells preached long and hard when there was a funeral service. They reminded everyone that they were headed for the grave just like the one laid out in the casket and that they would stand before their maker to be judged. And then they told how righteous God is and how that sin of any kind cannot enter His presence—usually they named the sins too. They always scared everyone pretty bad. But about three-quarters of the way through the sermon, the cord, that had been holding the man down, broke. And the dead man sat straight up in his casket. The whole congregation ran, including the man's own family. But the preacher was hemmed in between the lively corpse and the back wall. Grandpa said that just as the last mourners were clearing the building, they heard the horrified preacher put a significant curse on a church with just one door.

By the time Diana and I were born, the old stone foundations were about all that was left of the Hard Shell's and Soft Shell's churches. Here and there, crumbling chimneys stood above the vines and briars, but the earth finally reclaimed almost all of it.

CHAPTER 5

POKE YOUR HEAD OUT RANDALL

One night while we were sitting around the fire talking and singing and waiting for Mother and Daddy to come pick me up, Grandpa told us how the Robinettes came to be living in America. He said they left northern France in the 1600's with the Huguenots who were being persecuted by a Catholic king. The Robinettes were Protestants. They went to Ireland where they heard about William Penn's doctrine of toleration. So in 1682 they moved again—this time to join Penn in his "holy experiment" in America. From Pennsylvania, they moved south to Richmond, Virginia and then moved inland and settled down for good in the Appalachian mountains. Grandpa told the story real slow, explaining every detail because, I believe, he meant for us to remember it. When Grandpa finished the story, I looked at Diana and she looked as amazed as I felt. I guess we had never even wondered before that time where our families came from. They had probably come to America from all over the world. The farthest I had ever been from home was to Bent Mountain. Daddy said that was about one hundred and seventy-five miles away. I thought it was clean out of this world.

Diana and I started wondering what France and Ireland looked like. I got a sneaking suspicion that Grandpa and Grandma figured that story would get our interest up because when Mother and Daddy took me back to their house the next morning, Diana and I found a book on the kitchen table with a lot of maps and pictures and history in it. We spent the next week tracing our ancestors all over Europe and making up stories about them.

We asked Grandpa to tell us more stories about his family and he told us that his Daddy, Henry, fought in the War Between the States. He wasn't old enough to fight because he was only sixteen when the war broke out. But he lied and told them he was "of age." He had to run away from home to join because his mother, Annie, wouldn't let him go. Many of the mountain people didn't want to get involved in the war. Grandpa said that was on account of Mountain people didn't have a cause to fight for in that war like they did in the Revolutionary War. In the Revolutionary War, it was the mountain people that were the first to rally when Washington called for troops. And it was the mountain men's rifles that won over the old English Blunderbuss. Grandpa said that Mountain men had to have guns that shot straight on account of living off the land the way they did. So they asked the German gunsmiths to come up with something that could shoot a squirrel out of a tree. The German gunsmiths lengthened the barrels and rifled them out so the bullets would spin. And it was that American rifle that won the war.

But when the War Between the States broke out, the mountain folks were in a dilemma because they didn't know anything about the problems between the North and South because the mountain people just barely had enough of everything for themselves. And most of them didn't own any slaves and didn't believe in slavery either. They were slaves themselves—slaves to the mountains. Grandpa said that the mountains had a way of "equaling" people. And anyhow, the Scotch-Irish that settled the mountains were independent sorts. They didn't want to rule anybody and they didn't want to be ruled by anybody. That's why they picked a part of the country no one else would live in and that they thought the government wouldn't come poking around in. It was told, Grandpa said, that even the Indians knew better than to live there. The Cherokees carried out hunting expeditions into the area but they found the living easier in the Great Smokey Mountains.

Once the War Between the States broke out, though, mountain people felt forced to choose sides. Most of them felt more Southern than they did Northern and anyway they had to try to protect, from northern invaders, what little they had scratched out of the mountains. But still, there were a few brothers who chose different sides and fought against each other. Henry fought for the South. Grandpa said that after Henry went off to fight, Mathias got word one day that some northern troops were headed that way and they were looting and burning. Annie had soup beans cooking on the stove, and corn bread baking in the oven. Mathias told her to scatter the beans and bread in the yard cause he weren't feeding no Yankee invaders. Then Mathias and Annie took the children and headed for the hills. Finally, Henry got home safely and he married Mary on Jan. 4, 1865 and they raised a family of eleven children including Grandpa.

Grandpa said that things changed a lot after the war. Outsiders came into the mountains and bought up, and practically stole, land and mineral rights from the people. Then they punched holes all in the mountains to get at the coal, leaving open wounds everywhere. He said the coal companies built whole towns around each coal mine for the miners to live in, and they imported people to work and separated the housing by race and nationality. Grandpa said it created some hard feelings twixt the people for a while. But, he said, when men worked in the coal mine all day long on their hands and knees digging that old black coal, not even God could tell them apart when they came out. Grandpa looked right at me and Diana and said, "Around the coal mines—the ground is always level."

Diana and I always managed to get Grandpa back on the subject of Henry and there were plenty of good stories because

Henry loved to joke and kid around all the time. Grandpa said that when he and Jim and Mac, Grandpa's twin brothers, were little boys they asked Henry about the war. "Were you in the battle of Bull Run?" they asked. Henry said that he was. "Well", Grandpa said, "did you run?" "I'm here, ain't I?" came Henry's reply. I wished we had known Henry for ourselves. But hearing about him from Grandpa was the next best thing.

Grandpa said that Henry always carried his twenty-two shells in his pocket along with his twist tobacco for his pipe. One day when he filled his pipe with tobacco he didn't realize it but he put a twenty-two shell in there too. After he lit the tobacco, the pipe blew into a hundred little pieces and all he had left in his mouth was the stem.

Once, when Henry had to go pick up some extra supplies, he went to the barn to fetch his mule to ride but somebody had borrowed the old mule to plow with. Not to be outdone, Henry got the steer instead, climbed on, and pulled its tail up over his shoulder. Then he rode it all the way to Russell County.

Diana and I figured Henry for quite a character and Grandpa said we were right. He told us that people said that when Henry died they didn't know where he'd go because he was too good for heaven and too ugly for hell. Grandpa said that Henry nor his brother, Randall, neither one, were known for their good looks, and one time they were both heading to Abingdon in Henry's wagon. Henry was driving and Randall was in the back of the wagon amongst some straw and chicken feathers, asleep. A man stopped Henry to ask directions and then said to him that he believed he was the ugliest man he ever saw in his life. Henry bet the man five dollars he could show him somebody even uglier. The man took him up on it. Henry turned to the back of the wagon and hollered, "Poke your head out, Randall." Randall roused up a little and opened one eye and poked his head out of the wagon. Of course he had straw and chicken feathers all in his hair. The man took one look and handed Henry the five dollars. Easiest money he ever made in his life, Henry said.

Grandpa said that even after Henry was an old man, he was still full of pranks. On the day that he turned ninety years old he got on his mule and started down to the store on Dry fork. On the way he met Ted Brooks. Ted offered Henry a little horn of liquor and Henry wasn't above taking a snort or two every now and again so he drank a little and then sat down by the road to talk with Ted a while. By the time Henry started on his way again, the drink had begun to take effect and Henry bet Ted five dollars that he could run and jump on his mule from behind. Well, Henry ran up and placed his hands on the mule's hind quarters and sprang into the air and sailed clean across the top of the mule's head and landed on the road. That was good enough for Ted Brooks so he handed the ninety-year-old man his five dollars.

Henry had the name for being one of the country's best horse traders and could talk anybody out of whatever it was of theirs that he wanted. When Henry's family was all grown and married off, Henry accompanied Mary to church one Sunday as usual, but that particular Sunday he got saved. Two weeks later, when the family was all gathered in for Sunday dinner, Mary asked the boys if they hadn't seen a great change in Henry. Mac, the twin son who Henry had just traded out of a good milk cow, spoke up and said, "Yeah, bad to worse, bad to worse."

Henry liked to tell jokes and he always used the names "Pat" and "Mike" for his characters. Henry said Pat took a notion to get himself a girlfriend. But he didn't rightly know how to go about it, so he asked Mike. Mike told him to pick out a girl that he thought was real pretty and then think of something that he liked more than anything else in the world—something sweet and good that he liked to eat. Then Mike told Pat to take the girl in his arms and call her by that sweet name. Pat picked out the prettiest girl he could find and walked straight up to her and said, "Come into my arms, dried apples."

Henry said that besides courting, Pat and MIke liked nothing better than going a-hunting. On one of their expeditions, they saw a tree with a big hole in it and heard a noise inside, so Mike climbed the tree to see what it was. He saw that it was a cub bear in the tree and they allowed it would be nice to take it home and pet it. About the time Mike crawled into the hole to fetch the cub, the old mama bear heard all the commotion and came back and commenced to climb the tree. Well, Pat grabbed the mama bear by the tail just as she got her head into the hole. Mike didn't know what had happened so he hollered at Pat, "What darkened the hole?" Pat, holding on for dear life, yelled back, "Tail holt slips, you'll see what darkened the hole."

After stories like these, I started giving more thought to my heritage. I wondered if my great grandparents liked papaws and persimmons and sassafras tea the way I did. I wondered which one of them enjoyed getting up early and watching the sun's first rays run across the ridge. I wondered if they liked to read poetry, and dig their toes in creek banks. I wondered if Annie liked butterflies and little pigs and I wondered what stories she made up at night as she watched the flames of the fireplace jump and dance and shudder and sink. And I wondered what Henry might have said when he got caught in a hail storm. I liked these new thoughts and feelings and I could tell that Diana was thinking them too; we just didn't know how to talk about it. But every now and then when we were playing, one of us would holler, "Poke your head out Randall." That would be worth five to ten minutes of laughter.

The only bad thing was Grandpa's sickness. He took spells where he couldn't hardly breathe. Grandma mixed whiskey and honey and gave to him. Some nights it didn't help. He coughed and just kept coughing without getting his breath. Those were the nights when I learned how to pray in earnest.

Grandpa Mullins told us stories during the day while Grandpa Robinette was at work. His stories were about his early life. Grandpa's wife, who died way before I was born, was Nannie Davis. Nannie's daddy was Jess Davis. Nobody remembered much about him because he and his wife decided to move to Oregon after all their children married and left home. They begged Nannie to let Bessie, my grandmother, go with them. But Nannie refused. After they loaded up their wagon and left, none of the family ever saw them again. Nobody knew why they wanted to take Grandma instead of some of her brothers and sisters. But Diana and I agreed that it was for the best that she didn't go because the two of us might never have seen the light of day, and life sure was good.

CHAPTER 6

ROUGH SIDE OF THE MOUNTAIN

Grandpa Mullins didn't have any idea where his parents came from besides Kentucky. Grandpa grew up in a one room house on the rough side of the mountain not far from Elkhorn City, Kentucky. The house had a flat roof and both ends were open—sort of like a cracker box. In the middle of the room was a fireplace almost as long as the room itself. When they needed another log for the fire, they went out and hitched a log to the mule and drove him into the house in front of the fireplace, unhitched the log, and drove the mule through the other end. When he got through telling us about where he grew up, Grandpa said, "Pon my word and honor children, it's every word the truth." We liked that. Grandpa Mullins said that about everybody in the mountains carried knives and guns, not to hunt or whittle with—to kill with. He said people were awful mean back then in that area of Kentucky and Virginia. Pound was a little border town in Virginia just across the mountain from Kentucky. He said that on a Saturday night, in Pound, you could see to stab a man by the light of the gunfire. Then Grandpa looked into the fireplace and stared like he was looking a long way off. Finally he said, "Children, when you grow up on the rough side of the mountain, you learn to survive." Grandpa squinted his little beady eyes out from under that shiny bald head and turned and looked straight at me and Diana. "Children, you've come from a long line of survivors what never knowed the meaning of fear. So no matter what happens, don't never give up ner quit. Pon my word and honor, don't never give up."

One time, though, when Grandpa Mullins was a little boy going to Pound with his uncle Ira Mullins and some other Aunts and Uncles, he almost didn't survive. That's when the Red Fox and his gang attacked and killed everybody but Grandpa and one aunt. "Pon my word and honor, children," he said, "we was about to the top of the mountain when they struck. Bullets was a-zizzing every which way. Me and Nancy Jane, uncle Wilson Mullins' wife, was behind the wagon, she was riding a mule. She jumped off the mule and grabbed me and we hunkered down behind a clump of bramblebushes to hide. I was twelve years old at the time. After them thieving rascals shot and killed purt near everybody, they commenced to go through their clothes for money. When Doc Taylor, the Red Fox, come upon Louranza, my uncle Ira's wife, he throwed her dress over her head and taken his big knife and split her petticoat where she kept her money sewed into it. When he did that, he ripped her thigh wide open from her hip clean down to her knee. She just laid there and bled. Doc Taylor didn't care for nothing, he didn't. After they holp theirselves to everything worth taking, they rid off unconsarned and Nancy Jane went for the sheriff. But I run every step of the way back home. Pon my word and honor children, that's the way it happened."

That night when Mother and Daddy came to take me home, Grandma let Diana spend the night with me. But we didn't sleep. We were busy asking about the Red Fox. We found out that he also put himself up as a preacher and a doctor—doctoring the mountain people with herbs. He was hung in 1893 at Wise for the very crimes Grandpa Mullins described to us.

Daddy told us that Grandpa Mullins himself had learned to be right handy with knives and guns—growing up the way he did. Daddy had talked to a man in Elkhorn City one time and he told Daddy that when John Mullins and his own daddy were young, them and some of the other boys played on the sandbars of the river that flowed through the breaks in the mountain. They would run at each other and butt heads until only one was left standing. And that one was declared the champion. The winner of that game was always John Mullins. They got to calling him Bull Headed John. After the man in Elkhorn City told Daddy that story, Daddy asked Grandpa if he had ever heard of Bull Headed John. Grandpa smiled and said, "Pon my word and honor, that was me."

One more story was all that Daddy got to tell us about Grandpa Mullins that night because Mother said we just had to get to bed and get some sleep. But we might as well have stayed up, for all the sleep we got.

"After John," (Daddy called Grandpa Mullins "John") "was grown and married, he still kept his guns and knives handy just in case there was ever any trouble. One night he heard squawking in his chicken house and he grabbed his gun and went to see what was wrong. He saw two eyes look up at him so he shot at them and then he heard a groan and a thud. He saddled up his mule and rode to town and told the sheriff he had shot a man trying to steal his chickens. On the way back, John explained to the sheriff that he wouldn't a-shot the thieving rascal atall excepting that the man made at him with a knife. When they got back to the scene of the murder, they found John's best milk cow lying dead beside the chicken house." I wished Grandpa could have been there when Daddy told that story. I figured he would have said, "Pon my word and honor, children, if it ain't ever word the truth."

Sometimes, at night, Grandpa Mullins and Grandpa Robinette got to playing banjos for us. Grandpa Mullins played the claw-hammer banjo while Grandpa Robinette played the five-string. They played "Going up Cripple Creek." And we sang:

Going up Cripple Creek
Going in a run
Going up Cripple Creek
To have me some fun.

Diana and I told them they had been up Cripple Creek, they were on their way back down now. The other song we liked best was about a drunk man. Grandpa Robinette taught us the words:

I came home the other night drunk as I could be
Found a head a-laying on the pillow where my head ought to be
Come here wife, my little wife, explain this thing to me
How come aheads laying on the pillow where my head ought to be
You blind fool you crazy fool can't you never see
That is just a cabbage head your granny gave to me.

I've traveled this world over a thousand times or more
And a mustache on a cabbage head I never have seen before.

The song had a lot of verses and Diana and I learned all of them. Mary and Delmer and Grandma sang the songs with us too. What a time we had.

Grandma Robinette let Diana stay with me at Grandma Hall's house some of the time. Grandma had a rocking chair on the front porch. Every day, after all the chores were finished she headed for the porch. On the way, she always stopped at the hall mirror and replaited her long white hair and wound it on the back of her head, holding it in place with hair pins. Then she carefully replaced the two silver combs just above the plaited bun. Satisfied with her appearance, she went to the porch and rocked back and forth in that rocker and pinch-pleated the hem of her apron. She'd let it out and pinch-pleat it again while she watched the "many shades of evening." Diana and I gave the swing a push then pulled our feet up into the seat. The rocker knocked against the planks on the floor as Grandma rocked, and the swing squeaked as it got slower and slower and it all seemed to be in complete harmony with the frogs and whippoorwills and other evening sounds. Sometimes, when we didn't have anything else to do, Diana and I figured the temperature by listening to the crickets. Grandpa Robinette had told us to count the number of chirps in 14 seconds and add forty to it and that would tell us the temperature. It always worked too. We checked it by the thermometer Grandpa Hall had nailed to the smoke house. But Diana and I couldn't figure out why telling the temperature was so important to crickets.

When it rained, Grandma sat on the porch in the rocking chair and told stories about a boy named Jack or sang ballads.

She didn't sing the popular mountain songs. She sang the sad old ballads that all sounded alike except for the different names. She sang about Barbara Allen and Pretty Polly and Darling Cora and Molly Vaughn. Diana and I learned every word to the songs. We sat in the swing and Grandma gave each of us a quilt to cover up with because sometimes it got chilly in the mountains when it rained.

Grandpa Hall usually sat in a cane chair on the porch and got a mealy apple and peeled it. Then he took his knife and scraped the apple and ate it like apple sauce. He made it look so good that Diana and I ate our apples that way too. Of course, apples attract bees and we had to learn the difference in stinging bees and good news bees. You want good news bees to hover and hum around you and if one lands on you it's even better. Although Grandpa ate apples and other food, he couldn't actually taste anything. He was gassed in the Black Forest of Germany during World War I and spent a year in Walter Reed Hospital in Washington D.C. when the war was over. They didn't think he was going to live. He lived, but he never could smell or taste anything after that. And sometimes his throat swelled up until he couldn't hardly breathe. A man from Wise, that was in the war with Grandpa, told Daddy that while they were waiting to be shipped to the front lines to fight, the army had them play a game of soccer one day. Grandpa was a big man, over six feet tall, and stout back then too. So when he started down the field with the soccer ball, the man said, no one had better get in his way if they valued their lives. The Sargeant talked to Grandpa about playing too rough and hurting people. Of course, Grandpa knew nothing about games like that, growing up the way he did. So when the Sargeant told him to play the game right, Grandpa told the Sergeant that he didn't come there to play no games. He come there to fight a war, and get it over, and go home. And Grandpa did make it home, but not without paying the price.

Diana and I were so interested in finding out where everyone came from that we asked Grandpa Hall who his ancestors were. Grandpa didn't know where his family came from except Hall Holler on Dry Fork. Grandpa's father was "Uncle" Johnny Hall and his mother was Rosa Stallard, the daughter of Cyrus Stallard. Rosa was Uncle Johnny's second wife. His first wife died. He said that, among other things, Uncle Johnny made moonshine for a living. He made a good grade and people came from all over Wise County to buy his shine. He was one of the first in the area to offer a delivery service for the stuff. He never got caught by the law either, because he figured out a good system. He sold milk and eggs too. So he and Rosa delivered the milk and eggs and moonshine together. But he painted all of his jugs white and set the moonshine in the wagon amongst the buttermilk and eggs. If ever the law checked him, it looked like he had a wagon load of milk and eggs. After Grandpa married Grandma they lived in Hall Holler a little while and then moved out because Grandma said she didn't cotton to no moonshining. Grandpa was glad to get away. Hall Holler and World War I hadn't been too good a start on life for him. He hadn't got anything but a third grade education because Uncle Johnnny didn't believe his children needed to learn anything more that a little reading and writing. Grandpa started first grade at Dry Fork School. But they had arithmetic class the first day and the teacher asked Grandpa to add two and two. Grandpa told the teacher he'd never heard tell of any such thing like that so the teacher asked Walker Hall to try it. Walker figured a long time on his fingers and finally got it right. Grandpa said he decided that if he had to take arithmetic class he wasn't going to school. So the teacher over at Pine on Bull Run told Grandpa that if he'd come over there to school he wouldn't have to learn arithmetic—reading and writing was all he'd have to take. So Grandpa walked across the mountain to Pine to get his education. Back then, Grandpa said, teachers got paid according to the number of students they had in school.

Grandpa said about the only thing he really enjoyed doing as a boy was going to Abingdon with his daddy about twice a year to fetch supplies. He said Uncle Johnny had always taken his brother, Walter, to Abingdon until Walter told Rosa on him for not saying grace before eating. Uncle Johnny and Walter had stopped at an inn about half way to Abingdon and sat down to supper when the lady who ran the inn asked Uncle Johnny if he said grace before meals. Uncle Johnny replied, "No mom, not often." When they got back from Abingdon, Walter told Rosa what Uncle Johnny said. From then on Uncle Johnny took Grandpa to Abingdon with him and Grandpa was careful to keep his mouth shut. Grandpa said he loved the trip to Abingdon because it took several days and they got to cross the north fork of the Holston river. In the summer, they crossed the river in a shallow spot, but in winter, they took mules and wagon across on solid ice.

CHAPTER 7

HAINTS AND HOOFENAUGERS

Grandma knew where her family came from. Her mother's family were Bonds. Her mother, Catherine Bond (Ma), married Wilson McCarty. Catherine's parents were Mary Lawson and James Bond, James Bond's parents were George Bond and Lucy Powers, and George Bond's parents were William Bond and Margaret Davis. The Bonds had been a rather wealthy family in England, Grandma said. They even had a street in London named after them. They rubbed elbows with Lords and Earls and the likes before they came to America. It sounded reasonable to me because everybody said that Grandma's family all had aristocratic noses. Grandma said it was told that the Bonds would have been among the first settlers in the new world but a storm bombarded the seas just before the ship reached land. The captain said they must throw everything overboard that wasn't necessary for the voyage. They threw over trunks full of clothing and valuables. The storm worsened and the captain said they must toss even more cargo into the sea. All they had left on board was food and whiskey. And when the whiskey went overboard the Bonds all went over after it. Grandma said that's why the Bonds didn't make it to the new world until the second shipload of settlers. Grandma laughed so hard when she told that story that she took her glasses off and wiped the tears from her eyes with her apron. We figured that tale must have undergone some serious exaggeration by the way she laughed.

Grandma said that her father's family were McCartys and that Mr. McCarty settled in Scott County. When Grandma got to that point she just trailed off and didn't say anymore. Grandpa said, "Tell them all of it, Cora. You started so you might as well tell them all of it." "Well," Grandma said, "I never did put any stock in such a story as that." But then she said that apparently Mr. McCarty was not a Puritan by any stretch of the imagination. "As a matter of fact," Grandpa said, "it was told that he took two wives, one of each color, and had children by both." But Grandma added right fast that the second wife didn't take his proper name so those children weren't known by McCarty. That seemed to satisfy her but Diana and I enjoyed sneaking a few grins and raised eyebrows at each other.

Grandma asked if she ever told us about working in the hainted house when she was a little girl. We said no but we sure wanted to hear all about it. Grandma said she was in the sixth grade when her daddy died of consumption from working in the coal mines. "Now I'll tell you all this," she said. "My daddy left this old world a-shouting cause he knew he was going to a place far better than this. But he left two little children who never sat down to a table again except they put the food there by the labor of their own hands. "Before Daddy died we'd never wanted for food. After he died, I watched my little brother, Jim, dip a bite of corn bread in some meat grease and eat it and then lick his plate for five minutes to make sure he had it all." Grandma said that was when she and Jim quit school to go to work. She said if she could have gone to school one more year—through sixth grade—they would have let her teach. But she and her younger brother, Jim McCarty, hired out to work for other people until they were grown. Her mother, Ma, couldn't work at that time because that was when she was "down" for three or four years. Grandma had older sisters but they were already married when their daddy died. And their baby sister, Little Minnie, died several years earlier when a cat got into the house and jumped on the bed where Little Minnie was sleeping and sucked the breath out of her body. That's why Grandma never liked cats.

Anyway, Grandma did the housework and cooking for people when there was a new baby in the family. One of the places she worked when she was almost grown, was at a house in Banner, for a Bruce family. She was given a room out by the kitchen. Every night after she went to bed a light passed by her window then the door to her room opened. Someone walked slowly into the room, leaving the door open to the outside, went straight to the little coal stove in the room and shook the grate. Then he left, closing the door behind him. Grandma said that while the door was open she could feel the cool air blowing into the room. The first night that happened, Grandma said she screamed for Mr. Bruce to come there right quick. Mr. and Mrs. Bruce told her there was nothing to be afraid of. It was only the old man who used to stay in that room and work for them. He was killed in a mine explosion at Greeno but he had returned each night after his death to fix the fire. Grandma said the door was locked from the inside before the haint arrived, and when the haint left, the door was locked from the inside again. She said that several times when she was real scared, Mr. Bruce allowed her to stay in the main house with the rest of the family until right late.

After Grandma told that story she said that she had worked like a brute all her life and God in heaven only knew how hard it was for her and her little brother Jim after their daddy died. But she said they weren't the only ones that were poor. She remembered one winter when she helped a widow woman heat rocks in the stove and wrap them in quilts. Then they took the rocks and her baby to the fields. They sat the baby on the rocks to keep warm while they picked wild greens. Grandma said the mountains always cradled a lot of orphans because mountain life was so dangerous, especially after the coal mines opened. But people took care of each other. The ones that had cows and chickens shared milk and eggs with them that didn't have any. The ones that had mules and oxen plowed the fields for the ones that didn't have the animals to do with. And they helped each other build barns and houses and make quilts. Knowing how to live off the land that way and helping each other out in time of need was how they survived, she said. But she said that the people brought in from other places by the coal companies were the hardest hit when the mines failed or when they got down sick. They didn't know how to live off the land. They didn't know what to gather to eat and they didn't know what herbs and roots and bark to gather for medicine. They would have died if the mountain people hadn't a-helped them out, she said.

Grandma's stories about how people used to live weren't all bad though. She told us about stepping it off at the barn dances, and about kissing at the corn huskings when they found a colored ear, and about the taffy pulls. And she laughed until she cried when she told us about the chivalries where they hid outside the windows of new brides and grooms. Then just as the lamp went out, they beat on pans and yelled and made enough noise to wake the dead. Diana and I still liked that ghost story best. We hadn't heard any ghost stories at Grandma Robinette's. And we always tried to get Grandma Hall to tell her stories on the front porch, in the daylight.

Grandma told us about the time Labourn Lawson got saved. His wife, Martha, begged him to go to church but he always found an excuse not to. One night when they were having a meeting at the Top of the Hill Church, Martha went and requested that everybody pray for Labourn that God would get a-hold of him. Grandma said everybody prayed until you could have heard them all over Dry Fork and Crab Orchard, and finally the meeting broke up and Martha went home. But when she got home she found the bedroom and bed in shambles and Labourn missing. Martha began calling for him and he came running in from outside. Labourn told her that just after he went to bed, something had got holt of him and wrestled him from the bed. He said he never had such a tussle in his life and thought he never would get shed of it. After giving him a good working over, the thing disappeared. He ran outside and hid until he heard Martha call. After that night, Labourn went to a "cottage" prayer meeting with Martha and professed salvation. He testified that "me and the old Massah have laid the tomahawk down."

One evening, Grandma told us that Uncle Bob Hughes, who lived on Dry Fork, used to walk about a mile and a half out of the mountain to catch a ride to the coal mine, so he had to leave home before daylight. One cold winter morning, Uncle Bob met a woman in a long white robe walking toward him. When she got close enough for him to see her face by his carbide lamp, she disappeared. He said she had long red hair reaching below her waist. He met her at the same place each morning. At first, he said, he was so scared he actually thought he was going to faint. She got so close to him, he said he could have reached out and touched her. But she didn't try to do him any harm; she just looked a little sad. After several weeks of that, the woman quit showing up. Bob said he felt a deep loss, the way he would have missed a member of the family.

Grandma said Uncle Bob's haint was probably the same woman seen by a lot of mountain folk for many years. She stalked the hills and hollers, always dressed in a long white (or sometimes black) robe or gown, and approached people as though she needed to tell them something. But when she got close enough and was just about to speak, she always disappeared.

Diana and I didn't know if we would like to meet the mountain ghost woman or not. Diana said she must have been looking for the right person to tell her story to. As much as I enjoyed stories, I still hoped she wouldn't pick me.

One evening we were sitting on the porch listening to the swing and rocker tap out their rhythm, when Grandma told us that there used to be black panthers and hoofenaugers and all kinds of unusual snakes in the mountains. She said that when she was a girl, people told about hoop snakes that would stick their tails into their mouths and roll down the hill toward their prey. And there were black racers that wrapped people and killed them. But a black racer could only chase you down hill. So you had to turn and run back up hill to get away from one. Then there were the black snakes that could charm people. Grandma said she was told of a little girl who was charmed by a black snake that had come inside and was living on the family's hearth. The parents wondered why the little girl always took her supper to the fireplace to eat. One day they saw the little girl feeding a blacksnake. She was saying "one bite for you, and one bite for me." The distraught parents killed the black snake but then, of course, the little girl died because if a black snake charms someone and the snake is killed, the charmed person dies too.

And Grandma told us that people always said you better stay away from bats because they were as dangerous as snakes. If a bat lays eggs in your hair, you'll go crazy, she said.

I had heard a lot of people talk of black panthers and hoofenaugers and had even heard people tell about being chased by them. Grandma said she always believed that a hoofenauger was what Grandpa saw once when he was a young man. Grandma told us the story but every now and then she asked Grandpa if that was how it went and he verified every detail of it. Grandma said that one night Grandpa and his brother, Walter, were walking two girls home from church. Grandpa walked his girl home and started back to his house by himself. From where the girl lived, he had to cross a hill to get to Hall Holler. Running along the top of the hill was a rail fence. Just as Grandpa got to the fence, a strange four-legged creature, with pointed ears, human-like eyes, and a long tail, jumped upon the fence beside him and blew out the light of his lantern. Then, when Grandpa reached the head of the holler above his house, a ball of fire came over his head from out of the sky and hit the ground in front of his feet. Later, Uncle Mark, one of Grandpa's brothers, shot and killed himself in that very spot. Grandma said that the hoofenauger and the ball of fire were warnings.

Those stories scared Diana and me so much that we wouldn't go to the toilet after dark by ourselves, for the rest of the summer.

Grandpa Hall had another brother, Lilburn, who also killed himself but it had nothing to do with hoofenaugers. It was because he grieved over the loss of his wife and children. Lilburn married Hallie Kennedy from Caney Ridge and they had eight children. Hallie took sick and died and Lilburn was struggling to work and take care of the children too. Some of the people of the Freewill Baptist church on Dry fork decided to take his four youngest children and put them in the Freewill Baptist home in Greenville, Tennessee. So they came and got Richard and Raymond, the nine-year-old twin boys; and Ellen and Bonnie, the baby girls. Grandpa said Lilburn never was the same after that. One day, however, Lilburn loaded up in his old model-T Ford and headed for Greenville to fetch his children home. When he got there, he turned the car and parked it outside the door with the engine running. He intended to grab the children and run. But when he got back home empty-handed, he said that orphanage workers held on to the children the whole time he was there and he had to come back without his babies. After he told that, Grandpa said, he walked into the woods and shot himself. When that story was over, Diana and I got Grandma to telling more ghost stories just to take our minds off the sadness.

That night, I asked Mother why Grandma and Grandpa Robinette didn't have any ghost tales to tell. Mother said that some people believed in ghosts while other people perpetuated the belief in their existence. She said Grandma Robinette was one who perpetuated their existence. She told Diana and me that when Grandma Robinette was a teenage girl she lived near a house that a lot of people thought was haunted. One day she went to visit the lady who lived there. When she arrived, she heard the lady doing some work upstairs. The stairway went up from an entrance hall and had a closet underneath it with a sheet hanging over the door. Grandma decided to have a little fun so she hid in the closet. When she heard the lady start down the stairs, Grandma began to moan and push the sheet out. It scared the lady so much, she fainted and rolled down the rest of the stairs. Then Grandma got scared because she thought the lady was dead. She ran to the barn and told the lady's husband to come quick, something was wrong with his wife. She told him that she found his wife lying in the floor at the bottom of the stairs. By the time they got to the house, the woman had revived and began telling them about the haint she saw. The woman went to her grave thinking she saw the ghost that the house was supposed to harbor. She told the story over and over—even told it years later to Grandma, who kept her mouth shut.

Diana asked why Grandma Robinette didn't believe in ghosts when so many people did. Mother said that it wasn't the dead that Grandma had to worry about when she was growing up, it was the living. Grandpa Mullins was so mean to the children that once they survived him, they feared nothing or no one. She said that Grandma and her brothers and sisters wanted to go to school but Grandpa Mullins beat them and told them they didn't need no learning. Grandma worked for neighbors and used the money to buy school books but Grandpa Mullins found the books and burned them and beat her worse than ever. From then on, she hid in the chicken house to read her books and practice writing. Mother said that the only peace the family saw was on the occasions when Grandpa left home and stayed gone for months at a time. Once, when Nannie, his wife, asked him to fetch some coffee from the store, he left and didn't come home for a whole year. And when he finally returned, he walked into the house, and without saying a word, set the can of coffee on the kitchen table.

Here was another mystery to me. So I asked how come Grandpa Mullins was living with Grandma Robinette and she was taking such good care of him after he beat her when she was a little girl. Mother said that Grandma knew that Grandpa treated his own children the way he had been treated when he grew up. He didn't know any other way. So she didn't hold it against him. And anyway, she married into Grandpa Robinette's family and they were Hardshell and Freewill Baptist people and believed in being good to everyone and they were kind to Grandma and loved her like one of their own. Grandma chose that over the rough life she had grown up under. I understood right then and there why Grandma didn't like to see anybody whip their children. Also, Mother said that in his later years, Grandpa Mullins went to church with Grandma and Grandpa and was saved. After that, he was a whole different person.

Mother said that Grandpa Mullins outlived two wives. After Nannie died, Grandpa married again. He was in his 70s and he and his second wife had two more children, a girl and a boy. The census taker came through one day and just like he asked everybody else in the county, he asked Grandpa if he would swear that those were his children. Grandpa studied a minute and then replied, "No sir, I wouldn't swear to anything." The census taker put them down as Grandpa's children anyway, and went on about his business.

One of Grandma Hall's sisters visited with us one evening that same summer. Diana and I asked her something we'd been pondering—why the Bonds didn't take care of Grandma and her brother Jim after their daddy died. Grandma's sister said families usually took care of each other, especially when a father died and left little children. But the Bonds didn't want Ma to marry into the McCarty family in the first place. When Ma married Wilson McCarty anyhow, her family sort of withdrew. The bonds did help Ma's family occasionally after their daddy died, but not as much as they would have had Ma married somebody they approved of. And that was why Grandma and Jim had it so rough as they come up, she said.

That was late in the summer, and all too soon the day came when Uncle Ralph and Aunt Grace, Diana's daddy and mother, came to take her back to Norfolk. It was close time for school to start again. But it was a summer we wouldn't forget as long as we lived. We both said so.

There was something that happened to me that summer and I think it happened to Diana too. Before then, it was like I had my own little pool in the river that I could look into and always see my reflection. But that summer I was guided up river to the mouth, and on the way, I looked into many pools and saw the reflections of many people—ones who had already made the passage. Strangers who were part of me. After that, I didn't just see me when I gazed into my pool. I saw them too. It was then and there that I began to understand why life can be mysterious. But I still didn't have it all figured out.

CHAPTER 8

GOD'S UNCHANGING HAND

Just before school started back, the doctor said my health was so much better that I could start behaving normally. I was sure glad to hear that. I wanted to sleigh ride again.

One evening that winter when I went by Pansy's house, Mother asked me to stay with Pansy while she took her mother and grandmother to trade. People still said they went to trade because it hadn't been too long since they used the barter system. Back early, they didn't have cash money so they traded or bartered for everything they needed.

As soon as they left, I decided to try this notion I'd been working on for a while. I asked Pansy if she would like to sleigh ride. I don't think I ever saw her smile so big. I ran home as fast as I could and got my sleigh. It hadn't occurred to me that since Pansy didn't get out much in the winter, she didn't have many warm clothes. But I got a quilt and wrapped around her the way Mother and Daddy had done me when I was sick. Pansy was heavier that I thought she should be but I finally got her out the door and onto the sleigh. I sat her up and she held onto the sides with her hands and I tucked the quilt around her and pulled her to the top of Churchhouse Hill. Then I sat down on the sleigh in front of Pansy and pulled her arms around my waist so she could hold on to me. Then I put my feet on the guiders and pushed the ground with my hands to get started. I held on to the sides once we got going. It was actually pretty easy. I was surprised no one had thought of it before.

We flew down that hill. At first, Pansy was quiet. Then she was screaming and laughing at the same time. We were nearly to the bottom of the hill when a curious thing happened. An older-like couple by the name of Salyers lived right beside the road. They had a dog but he had never paid any attention to sleigh riders before. But this time, that big hound ran at the sleigh barking and grabbing at Pansy and me like he was mad or something. I should have just kept going. But I started yelling at him and then I tried to steer out of his way. As I veered to the left, one runner hit some deeper snow and the sleigh tried to turn over. Pansy must have turned loose of me because she wound up in the ditch in the curve. As soon as I felt her let go of me, I rolled off the sleigh and ran back to see about her. I grabbed her in my arms and looked to see how bad hurt she was but to my surprise she looked at me and laughed. Her face was skinned up but, besides that, she wasn't hurt. I got the sleigh and put Pansy back on it and started home with her. I don't know where the dog went. He must have gone home after he wrecked us. I took the little path through the woods by the spring and got Pansy home before my mother got back with her mother and grandmother. I heated some water and washed off Pansy's face. Then Pansy put her little fist beside her face and patted her temple. Directly she looked up at me and said, "It seemed like the right thing to do." We laughed so hard we almost forgot about the trouble we were in. For we knew we'd have to come up with something good to tell everybody.

Well, we couldn't think of anything but the truth and it sure didn't go over too good with them. They reckoned that I could have killed Pansy with such foolishness. Pansy's grandma got out the jar of Rosebud salve and smeared that pink stuff all over Pansy's face. She looked funny and I would have laughed except that her grandma gave me a mean look every time she smeared some on. Mother told Mrs. McCarty that she would bring some balm of Gilead salve she'd made last year, and then we started to leave. But just as Mother and I were going out the door, I looked back at Pansy and she winked and smiled real big at me. It didn't matter to Pansy that she skinned her face. She got to ride a sleigh one time and I reckon that was worth the hurt. Still, Mother said that I couldn't go back to Pansy's house or anywhere else, except school, for a week, so I would have time to reflect on my actions.

Somehow, word of the incident got around faster than fire in a hay loft and everybody I saw told me what a dumb thing I did. Nobody seemed to be mad at that hound. They blamed the whole thing on me. I felt lower than an egg-sucking dog. I figured that if I lived to be one hundred, I'd never understand grown people. But, after a little while, it was never mentioned again. I went on sleigh riding with the other kids as usual while Pansy sat home and read her books.

That spring when it warmed up enough, Pansy's grandmother let her sit outside in a chair and we read books together and wrote little poems. We watched the squirrels play in the trees and sometimes caught a glimpse of some deer at the edge of the woods. But for some funny reason Pansy loved the wind best. She liked to feel it blow her hair across her face and she liked to watch it swirl through the trees. She said that butterflies ride warm winds to heaven. And she pointed out how dear lean into the wind when they walk. I believe she could actually see it, the wind that is. I could only hear the shuffling leaves and the creaking of the big oaks as they swayed.

One summer day, Pansy and I were sitting outside and I told her I was going to run in the big race at the fair again. Pansy squirmed in her chair. Then she got this dead serious look on her face. She wasn't smiling or anything when she said, "Run like the wind, Geraldine, run like the wind." She just kept looking right at me until I felt my stomach do a somersault and we just stared at each other for a minute. Then I nodded and Pansy nodded and I knew what I had to do.

Daddy started helping me practice my running. He drove the Jeep out the road toward my grandmother's house and I ran along behind. As he drove faster and faster, I tried to keep up. I ran until my muscles ached at night. One morning I couldn't walk, my legs hurt so much, and Mother thought I had polio. She took me to Dr. Short in Norton. He told my mother later that when she first brought me in, he thought I had polio too. As it turned out, I had pulled some muscles in my legs. When we got home Mother built a fire in the stove and set the iron on it. Then she wet towels and put them on my legs and run the hot iron up and down the towels. I was running again the next day. I told Pansy about getting my legs ironed and she laughed so hard she almost fell out of her chair.

Pansy's grandmother gave her a watch with a second hand on it and my running became serious business for Pansy. I raced between two trees in front of Pansy's house and she checked how many seconds it took me to make it. I kept running harder, taking faster steps, lengthening my stride, moving forward, forward, forward. Then one day, for the first time ever, it happened. I was running out the road behind Daddy's Jeep when I felt my body become fluid. Every muscle, every cell, every atom in my body was flowing forward in one collective, effortless motion. I felt my toes tipping the ground as I melted into the air. When we got to my grandma's house, Daddy jumped out of the Jeep and yelled, "What in the world happened today? You were running like the wind." After the Possum Holler race I gave my blue ribbon to Pansy.

Everybody was still so excited after the fair that all of Possum Holler and most of Dry Fork were at the Top of the Hill that night. Lucy, Shirley and I got to the Top of the Hill before the crowd and climbed the trees behind the store and gathered mulberries. Then we took them inside and heated them on the stove so the worms would crawl out. Otherwise, you eat worms and all. We shared our feast with everybody as they came in and that put them all in an even better mood for stories. And I knew it was going to be a good night for stories; there was a tingle in my ears.

We didn't have enough chairs for everybody so us kids sat on the counter and on feed sacks. After a while I heard Uncle Victor say, "Why hello Labourn, how's ole Labourn a-doing?" Then Labourn said, "Why Vic Hall, you ole buzzard, what brought you out tonight?" Then I heard Labourn tell Uncle Victor that he was feeling tolerable and then he said, "Vic, I'm living on borrowed time, I wish to me die, I am." I knew Labourn meant that he was feeling okay but that he was living past his promised three score and ten years and so he could go at any minute. Labourn Lawson was one of the finest story tellers in the history of Wise County. Everybody said he was. but he was getting old and didn't come to the Top of the Hill but once every couple of months or so. I reckon he came when the stories inside him just couldn't stay put any longer and had to have an escape.

Everybody was getting their pop and cakes and finding a comfortable spot before the stories began. I got a grapette and a bag of potato chips. We were all moving around so much that it got the light bulbs to swinging on their cords and got the fly paper to swinging too. That threw funny lights and shadows across everything and made it look like people's noses were moving around, right on their faces. It was like a carnival in there. I had been to a carnival in Coeburn once when you could pay a quarter to see a petrified woman. But that wasn't the big carnival. I didn't go to the big carnival when Wadlow, the world's tallest man was there, because that was before my time. But all the men still talked about how Wadlow put a dollar bill on his head and anyone who could reach and get it, without jumping, could have it. The only person that came close was Beanpole Southerland from St. Paul.

Finally, Uncle Victor took a big sworp of his Dr. Pepper and cleared his throat and everybody knew it was time to commence.

"Some of you all remember when they built the road up to Pine Camp," Uncle Victor said. "Well, one of the men from Pine Camp who was a-working on the WPA had never seen nor heard tell of dynamite. They was a using dynamite to build the road—a-shooting out the rocks and stumps. Anyway, he decided he'd love to have him some of that dynamite to clear out his new ground. So he got some and stored it under the house and it got wet that winter and froze. In the meantime he had got him a battery radio. It wasn't much good—static was about all it got. But he loved to show it off and let people listen to what sounds he could get. And he kept it on all the time. About that time he decided to use his dynamite, but saw it was froze so he thought he'd have to thaw it out first. He had a little step stove in the house there, and he put his dynamite in the oven to thaw out. Well, along came his dad, down to listen to the radio. But all the static made his dad afraid it would blow up, so he warned his son to get rid of that infernal thing afore it blowed higher than a Georgia pine. His Dad left to go back home and just as he entered the door, the boy's dynamite blowed sky high and blowed the top of the stove clean through the roof of the house. His dad heard the explosion and told the rest of the family, 'Lord I warned that boy to get rid of that infernal radio afore it blowed up and plumb killed somebody.'"

Soc Holbrook was there that night and he started wiggling around in his seat a little and crossed and uncrossed his legs a

51

time or two. Then he fiddled with the metal snap on his galluses and opened his mouth like he was going to say something. I knew that meant he was just itching to tell a story. I guess everybody else knew it too because they all turned their attention on Soc and he knew he was next. So he commenced.

"By Ned"—By Ned was his word—"I was hitchhiking around the country once in my younger days and had got back to Bluefield—almost home—when it fell one of the galldarndest snows that was ever seen or heard tell of. So I decided to ride the train from Bluefield to Norton. The snow was piled so high on the tracks that it took five engines to pull just four coaches. The first four engines had to clear the snow. Well, by Ned, just as we turned a curve in a big cut, we come upon a prized milk cow standing smack dab in the middle of the tracks. She was the first registered cow to come to this area. A man had ordered her from out west and everyone from Bluefield to Norton knew about her. Course the engineer couldn't afford to hit that costly cow so he slammed on the brakes and stopped the train so sudden that it pitched all the passengers out of their seats to the seats in front of them, so that everybody had their heads in the seats and their rumps straight up in the air. Most of the passengers were women and of course their dresses was over their heads. The engineer, seeing all the commotion, authorized me to go through the train and pull the lady's dresses back down. Well, by Ned, they was a big stout woman in the last coach and I never seen such a rump on a human in my life. I pulled and tugged and struggled with her dress for nigh onto half an hour and liked to never got it back down. But, by Ned, I did get it, and when the engineer saw everybody was back in their seats, we was on our way to Norton."

By the time Soc got to the end of his story, Uncle Victor laughed so hard he nearly fell out of his seat and Uncle Maynard nearly choked to death on his moon pie. It was as much fun to watch everybody slap their legs and laugh as it was to hear the stories. Finally, I heard Labourn Lawson commence to clear his throat and just as I looked his way, he lunged right into his story.

"I Gonies," (that was his word) "back in the year of 1930, I think it was, a woman by the name of Elsie Carico got lost over in the Flat Woods a-picking huckleberries. I was commissioned to organize a search for her. By that time, she was so frantic that she was plum stone raving mad and run like a haint whenever she saw another human being. All the running through the brush and briars had tore every stitch of clothes off'n her body and, I Gonies, she was stark naked, I wished to me die, she was. I watched her for a while and noticed she was making the same circle all the time. So I hid behind a tree and when she run by, I just retch out and grabbed ahold of her."

"Labourn," Wallace Bond said, "Where did you grab her?"

"I Gonies, I grabbed her by the coat tail," was his reply.

It was a while after that one before everybody could get quieted down enough for the stories to begin again.

This time they got to telling bee tree stories. Well, Edgar Davis got it started off. He had cut a bee tree and got some ten gallon of honey out of it. Kendall Hall had cut one and filled ten warsh tubs. June Mead had gotten about fifteen barrels out of his last tree, and Wallace Bond got more than that and Allen Hale found two bee trees growed together. Uncle Victor stuck a spout into a bee tree once and got bucket after bucket of honey just like tapping a sugar maple for sap, and Clark Cassell was still eating honey he robbed from bumblebees ten years earlier, and Labourne got so much on the High Knob one time that it took several wagons to fetch it home. Everyone was satisfied. But as I said, on this particular night, everybody in Possum Holler was gathered in at the Top of the Hill, so Ballard Stallard was there too. Ballard had always been quiet. He listened and laughed at the stories but he never once told any. Well, just as everybody was swallowing another drink of pop, Ballard spoke up. "I went bee tree hunting once," he said. "You did," my Daddy said, looking up right quick. "Did you find one?" Yeah I found one, was all Ballard said. Looking a little impatient, Uncle Victor said, "Well tell us about it, did you get any honey out of it?" "Well no", said Ballard, "When I cut it, it fell in the river." You could see the disgust just eat its way around the room after such a story. After a while, Ballard commenced to speak again. "I don't know how much honey was in it," he said, "but it sweetened the river ten miles up and I don't know how far down."

That topped every bee tree story that had ever been told at the Top of the Hill. And to get topped by Ballard Stallard, who had never spun a yarn before in his life, was the worst kind of insult. Everybody headed back for Possum Holler. Labourn got in such a hurry, he didn't go the road but lit out across the hill and straight for his house, without a light or anything. I heard Mother and Daddy laughing about it for half the night after we got home.

Just before school started back, it was time for me to get ready for camp. I had never gone to camp before, although a lot of kids went because it was free. All you had to do was memorize Bible verses and you could go to Camp Bethel at Wise for a week. John Henry and some of his group came around to the schools about once a month with their flannel graphs and they told and showed Bible stories and John Henry performed his magic. He could pour milk into a hat and then put it on someone's head and it wouldn't spill out. And he could pour the red blood of Jesus into a black heart and it would turn the black heart as white as snow. There wasn't anything we loved better than a visit from John Henry. Well, that year during school, I memorized enough verses to go to Camp Bethel free. Mother helped me pack everything I'd be needing and drove me to Wise. I'd never been away from my family before. But it sure didn't seem like I was there a week because we sang and had Bible stories and we played games and swung on swings high in the air, and every day John Henry took us down to the swimming pool in Norton. And every night we sat around a bonfire and listened to Bible stories and ate more food, and most of us dedicated our lives to Christ. We stayed in cottages with bunk beds and I met a lot of girls my age. There were boys at camp too but they stayed in a cottage up the holler from us. The cottages were named Hither, Thither, and Yon. The only thing I was a little disappointed in, was the pool at Norton. It smelled like wash day at my house and it was too crowded. I was glad to get back to the Rock Hole, but it was a grand week.

Not long after I returned from camp, I knew winter was coming on again. I could tell because we packed the dairy with Mason jars filled with food, large stone crocks filled with pickled corn and beans and sauerkraut, and bushel baskets piled high with keeping vegetables and apples. Inside the house, in one large closet, hung sacks full of dried shuck beans and dried apples. And in the garden, cabbages had their heads stuck in the ground. Cabbage would keep clear past Christmas that way. And all the animals began to stir. Everyday, great flocks of geese stretched out like arrows over our mountains and valleys following the invisible paths laid down by their ancestors. Squirrels busied themselves with their winter homes. Deer flashed their white tails and darted into the laurel thickets. Leaves blushed and let go of their grip, tumbling to the ground. And the bittersweet smell of molasses-making filled the air.

And then it occurred to me that it wasn't real change at all, because it happened the same way every fall. It was just cycles. I was glad because I didn't like change.

I looked forward to winter because it hadn't been a good summer for selling coal. Sometimes Daddy had to leave his truck parked at the coal mine for three days before he could get it loaded. Daddy liked to load up with Widow Kennedy coal. It was the best grade, he said. Widow Kennedy left just a little bit of red ash when you burned it. Daddy said that all the coal in the mountains was bituminous coal which meant it was soft coal and good to burn. There was plenty of Shanon and jawbone coal at the mines. but Daddy always lined up his truck for Widow Kennedy. It was getting harder to sell coal too. When Daddy asked people if they'd be needing any coal, a lot of them said they wouldn't be needing any more coal, they'd done put in heat. Daddy said that meant they had put in oil or gas furnaces.

So that fall Mother and Daddy talked a lot about what they were going to do that winter. Mother had put up enough food to last all winter but they were thinking they wouldn't have money for anything else. I knew Daddy put his last two dollars in the offering plate that Sunday. It worried me a little but we had sung "Hold to God's Unchanging Hand," just before we dismissed church. That helped me feel better.

> *Time is filled with swift transition*
> *Naught of earth unmoved can stand*
> *Build your hopes on things eternal*
> *Hold to God's unchanging hand.*

Daddy started talking about going back to the coal mine again to work. And I think he would have too. But that night, right after Daddy started snoring, I heard Mother ease out of bed and go to the kitchen. I tiptoed in to see what she was doing; I found her on her knees by the window, the Bible beside her, and her hands folded in prayer. We had a green shade up at the window and it was raised, so a little light from the moon streamed into the room. But all around my mother was a white halo. I never saw anything like it. I knew that at that moment, God stopped whatever it was He was doing and attended to my mother's prayer. I went back to bed, but I couldn't get the picture of Mother out of my mind. Jerry Mays' wife had never looked so lovely. Then I remembered that Mother's hand still needed that ring and I intended to get it as soon as I could raise all of the money. I had saved up almost $50, mostly because gensing was bringing a lot. I lay still and thought about things a long time that night and I listened, but I never heard Mother go back to bed.

The next morning, right after breakfast, we heard somebody calling for Daddy from the yard. People always called from the yard. They didn't just walk right up to the door and knock. I don't know why that was. Mother and Daddy went to the door and saw preacher Wilson Addington standing out there, so Daddy told him to come on in and get a load off. He came into the house and after asking how everybody was and saying that he had been "fair to middling," he said, "James, I tell you why I come. You know I been selling for Watts Produce Company out Norton for a number of years now. But I been getting so many revival meetings here lately that I'm going to quit Watts and hold revivals full time. Some how or other I got you on my mind and decided I'd drop by and see if you'd be interested in the job." Daddy told him he sure did appreciate his asking and he would go that very day and see about it. After Preacher Addington left,

Daddy turned to Mother and said, "Wonder why in the world he thought of me for the job?" Mother just smiled and hugged him. I learned something right then and there: One night on your knees beats a winter's worth of worry. I thought of Buddy's favorite song:

> *Oh what peace we often forfeit*
> *Oh what needless pain we bear*
> *All because we do not carry*
> *Everything to God in prayer.*

CHAPTER 9

A REVIVAL THAT SET THE CHURCH ON FIRE

Daddy got the job with Watts Produce. At first he drove a produce truck and sold right off the truck. So every morning he had to go up to Watts and load the truck. Two days a week he had to get up at 2:15 a.m. Later, he took orders at stores and restaurants and brought the orders back to Watts and the next day someone else delivered what he sold. He worked all over Southwest Virginia and Eastern Kentucky. He liked the job because the more produce he sold, the more money he made. But it still wasn't as much money as he could make in a coal mine. So Mother decided to go to work at the sewing factory in St. Paul. Daddy sold his truck and bought a car to drive and Mother drove the Jeep to work. I hated to see the truck go. Daddy had taught me to drive it and sometimes he'd throw the keys to me and say, "Go turn the truck for me." I liked that. My Grandma Robinette started work at the factory at St. Paul too because Grandpa's breathing got worse and he couldn't dig coal any more. He had trouble just getting up the steps of their porch. He'd take a couple of steps and then have to stop and rest. I was afraid he might died of consumption like Grandma Hall's daddy, but I was scared to ask anyone if that's what he had. Anyway, Mother picked up Pansy's mother and Grandma Robinette and Aunt Mary and they rode together back and forth to work.

That left me to do the chores when I got in from school. I carried up our supply of cooking and drinking water from the spring. We had a barrel under the spout at the corner of the house and we used the water from it for other things. I soon learned to carry two buckets full of water at a time, instead of one, because it was easier to carry two. It was more balanced and didn't throw my body all out of whack. I even learned to swing a bucketful of water up over my head and back down without spilling a drop. And I noticed how handles on empty buckets sound a lot like guineas squeaking, except guineas are a lot louder. We had guineas to keep the bugs off the beans and potatoes and to keep the hawks away from the chickens. After I carried up enough water, I slopped the hogs and fed the dogs and chickens and guineas and coons and crow. The squirrel took care of himself. Sometimes I took the coons down to the creek and let them catch crawdabs. I wouldn't have thought it, but the coons were afraid of crawdabs. They would take one paw and raise a rock in the creek and carefully stick the other paw under it and feel around for crawdabs. Most of the time they got pinched. I sat on the bank and laughed at them. Daddy caught crawdabs for them when he took them to the creek. But I had been pinched too. So I didn't like to stick my hands under the rocks either. That's all the feeding I had to do because we had already sold our cow and got our milk and butter from Grandma Robinette.

After feeding, I carried in the coal and built a fire in the cookstove. Then I baked a pone of cornbread if we didn't have some left over from the night before. I could bake good corn bread. I learned how from Uncle Delmer the year I was sick. I got soup beans and greens and parsnips or potatoes and cabbage and green beans or peas and salsify out of the refrigerator and set them on the stove to warm. We called our salad "greens," because it was composed of all sorts of plants, herbs, and weeds. Every year, Mother and I made several trips to pick our wild greens. We gathered sweet and bitter cresses, plantain, dock, lambs quarters, poke, nettleweed, pusley, dandelion, sorrel, groundhog's ear and others. Mother canned enough of them to last until the next spring. Our green beans were White Half Runners, White McCaslan, Little Greasy Beans, Fall Beans, and in the winter—shuck beans, my favorite. I could eat shuck beans, pickled beets, and corn bread until I about exploded. Mother did the cooking on saturdays or in the evenings. After I finished my chores, I ran to Pansy's house and then in a little while Mother and Pansy's mother got in from work. Mother didn't have to help Pansy with her writing and reading any longer. Pansy was already doing book reports for the high school kids. Sometimes I got my sleigh and went to the Top of the Hill to join the other riders before Daddy got home. Daddy and I always polished the runners early in the fall and had her ready to go. After supper, Mother and Daddy and I either walked out to Grandpa Hall's house, or went back up to the Top of the Hill store, or to church. I liked this winter better than any other time in my life. If I could have made time stand still I would have done it right then.

One of the reasons I liked it so much was because Lucy, Shirley, and I got promoted to the older kids Sunday School class at church. That meant we got to go to youth meetings and act in the big Christmas play and help decorate the church for special occasions. I was feeling real grown up.

It was also the winter of our good revival meeting at the church. Wrightly Sallings was a preacher from Tennessee and he held a two-week meeting in the middle of February. The night he preached on hell, the church nearly burned down. Otherwise, it was like all the other meetings at our church. Mother and Daddy and Claude Hays and Beeb Lawson sang eight to ten songs every night to get it started off. And every night somebody, usually Foy Kern, requested that they sing "Cabin on the Hill."[1] And when they sang it, there wasn't a dry eye in the house. I learned every word of that song:

There's a happy childhood home
In my memory I can see
Standing out upon a hill
Neath the shadow of a tree
If I only had my wish
It would give my heart a thrill
Just to simply wander back
To the Cabin on the Hill.

Chorus

Oh I want to wander back
To the cabin on the hill
Neath the shadow of the tree
I would like to linger still
Just to be with those I love
Joy my heart would overfill
And I want to wander back
To the cabin on the Hill.

But the saddest of it all
I can never more return
To that happy childhood home
Matters not how much I yearn
But I have a better home
Where there'll never come an ill
Tis a mansion in the sky
And it stands upon a hill.

I cried along with everyone else every time they sang it.

Anyway, Wrightly Sallings started preaching and the first week he preached on heaven and the love of God. We had a lot of people saved that week. The second week, the weather turned colder than whiz and was way below zero every night. I remember it well because on Monday night it was so cold the caps blew off all the pop at the Top of the Hill store and everybody in Possum Holler had to help drink it so it wouldn't go to waste. But the crowds at church got larger and larger. We borrowed chairs from other churches and still had people standing in the back. The last week of the revival, Sallings preached on sin and Satan and the very last night he preached on hell. Now, everybody who had ever heard him preach said that when he preached on hell, it got piping hot in the church house.

1. <u>The Cabin On The Hill</u>, B.L. Shook (C) Copyright 1943 (renewal 1970) James D. Vaughan Music Publisher/SESAC a div. of Pathway Music, P.O. Box 2250, Cleveland, TN 37320 in <u>Sacred Thoughts</u>. Used by permission.

And they were right. The women fanned and everybody peeled off their coats and sweaters. The more he preached, the hotter it got. And the hotter it got, the harder he preached.

Finally, Daddy noticed that people were wiping sweat and fanning and almost gasping for breath and he decided that even if Sallings was preaching on hell, it shouldn't be that hot—not in that sub-zero weather. So Daddy slipped out the back door to check around and when he walked into the newly built basement, he saw it was on fire. Daddy hated to disturb the meeting, so he beat and stomped until he put out all the flames. Then he eased back into the meeting as if nothing had happened. Well, when Sallings gave the invitation, the mourner's bench filled up with sinners. I reckon they had experienced all the hell they ever wanted. And everybody said it was one of the best meetings they had ever had the pleasure of being a part of.

I liked church more all the time. I especially liked walking to church because we walked by Grandma Hall's house. Usually Grandma, Grandpa, and all my aunts, uncles, and cousins walked along together. In winter, Grandpa went early and built the fire so the church would be warm when everybody got there for the service. In the summer, my little cousins and I stopped and picked berries from the gooseberry and huckleberry bushes that grew along the path. Sometimes we could find dewberries or mountain tea berries.

And more than anything, I liked walking old paths. I liked placing my feet on the same good earth of my ancestors and pressing it down a little further, making the path a little deeper because I, too, had walked there.

That winter too, Mother and Daddy finally said I was old enough to sit with the bigger kids in church. Lucy and Shirley could too. We tried to keep quiet but we poked each other and pointed to funny things that went on. In the winter, especially, we watched for waspers.

During the week, when the church was cold, the waspers flew into the loft and sort of froze up. But when Grandpa built a fire in the stove for Sunday service, the waspers began to thaw out, and about midway through the service they poured out of the loft and commenced to circle up near the top of the high ceiling. Ever so often, one of them got dizzy and dropped like a rock. Usually it landed somewhere harmless but sometimes it went right down somebody's shirt or dress. It always caused a wonderful commotion.

Now that I was older, too, I enjoyed watching the little kids. They got to do something each week at the beginning of the service. The Sunday following our good revival meeting with Wrightly Sallings, some of my cousins sang a song that my aunt had taught them. They carried their books up to the front of the church and tuned up on a little whistle that came out of an oatmeal box. And they actually commenced to sing in that key. Then I noticed that one of them had her songbook upside down. She wasn't old enough to read but she wanted to hold a book anyway. They sang "I Feel Like Traveling On" and the words go: "My heavenly home is bright and fair, I feel like traveling on." But I distinctly heard, "My heavenly home is bright as fire." I thought that was a better version and considered writing and offering it to Stamps Baxter Music Company. Everybody enjoyed the service so much that it was almost disruptive.

The next Sunday, little Jimmy Belcher sang Amazing Grace and when he got to the verse: "When we've been there ten thousand years," he looked astonished and stopped in the middle of the verse and asked his mother, "ten thousand years?" His mother nodded. So he went on with the song.

That year too, Lucy, Shirley, and I got to help cut the Christmas tree and decorate. We always got a cedar tree. We called cedars "Christmas trees" because that's all we ever used for Christmas. And nothing in the world smells better than a cedar tree except maybe one thing, and that is sassafras tea boiling. Of course, not long after Christmas, it was time for sassafras tea. Because if you drink the tea in February, you won't get pneumonia for a whole year.

Anyway, we gathered holly and put it in all the windows and placed candles in the middle. And we put holly around all the old oil lamps on the wall. The hillside below the church house was thick with holly trees where holly had been thrown away after Christmas year after year. Of course, we always put a little mistletoe around. If the mistletoe wasn't too high in the tree, some of the boys climbed up and got it. If it was in the top of a tall tree, they'd shoot it out. That year, we found several big bunches of mistle toe in the top of a tree just above Clark Casell's house, and one of the boys shot it out. It fell on the ground and we made a dive for it and grabbed all we could and ran back to the church yelling and squealing. I think some of the boys were chasing a couple of the girls so they could hold the mistletoe over their heads. I wasn't sure, though, because I outran everyone back to the church. The mothers who helped with the decorations and the play laughed and had as good a time as we did.

After we decorated, we strung sheets in front of the stage for curtains. Our church and the churches on Dry Fork and Bond Memorial in Crab Orchard got together and scheduled the plays on different nights so everybody in all three communities could attend all the plays. After each play, Santa Clause entered the churchhouse and handed out presents and gave treats to everyone. The treat was a paper bag full of fruits, nuts, and candy. Santa always teased people and made the widow women and children hug him for their presents. And he always knew

Uncle Dan Ramey

**Mary Martin, Presbyterian missionary
to churches in Wise County**

Rev. Dan Graham revival meeting, Wise County, 1938

Aunt Catherine "Ma" McCarty with children
(left to right) **Cora, Norma, Jim, Lilly and Merril**

Diana Robinette, age 7

**The author, D. Geraldine Lawson, with parents
Anna Jean Robinette Hall and James J. Hall**

The Mt. Olivet Quartet
(left to right) **Claude Hays, Beeb Lawson, Jean Hall, James Hall**

some jokes to tell on the men and had everybody laughing. After it was all over, some of the boys shot firecrackers. Firecrackers were usually shot off on Christmas Eve but sometimes the boys got anxious and shot them after the plays. All the goings-on made Christmas my favorite time of year.

The other special thing about Christmas was that it was one of the few times that Pansy got to come to church. Several people usually put presents under the tree for her. No one ever knew who did it. That's the way it was with some of the presents. The widow women always got several unsigned presents too. The other presents under the tree were there because the Sunday School classes exchanged names.

We helped Pansy's mother and grandmother carry everything home. Pansy opened each present so as not to rip the wrapping paper. Then she folded the paper and put it and the ribbon in a box to save. She got handkerchiefs, a box of chocolate covered cherries, and a jigsaw puzzle with a picture of two kittens and a butterfly. Somebody got her a magic slate. It was the first one we ever saw. And she got a little fuzzy bear, a watch, and Chinese checkers. Then she opened my present—a book of poems by Emily Dickinson. Pansy ran her hand over the pages as if they were made of the finest silk. Then she reached her arms toward me and I bent down and she hugged me and I nearly cried. She hadn't ever hugged me before. Her mother told her she would have to put the book away until morning. It was getting late. When we left she was peeling an orange.

The next spring, things got right back to normal and we headed to the Top of the Hill and more pop and moon pies and tall tales. The store had just put in a penny bubble gum machine and the little round gumballs came in all colors. There were about two striped balls in the machine and anyone who got a striped one was paid a nickel for it. Then the lucky person could buy a bottle of pop with the nickel. Every night, all the children put pennies in the machine and everybody watched to see if they got a striped ball. That particular night, my little cousin, Kenny Robinette, Uncle Maynard's and Aunt Betty's oldest son, put his penny in and, low and behold, out rolled a striped ball. Everybody made over Kenny about his striped ball and finally he was offered a nickel. But Kenny, who was only five years old, had somehow gotten the impression that a striped ball was a prized worth hanging on to. So he refused to sell. Kenny's fascination with the striped ball amused everyone so much that they began to bid for the ball. Daddy offered him a dime and Uncle Victor offered him a quarter. Still, Kenny refused. Allen Hale offered him a fifty cent piece and Wallace Bond offered him a dollar bill. Kenny just stood there and shook his head. The bidding became more frantic and finally June Mead stood up, reached into his billfold and pulled out a five-dollar bill. He waved the bill toward Kenny and said, "Son, I'll buy that ball from you for enough money to keep you blowing bubbles to high school." But Kenny clutched the gumball inside his fist and crammed it into the very bottom of his pants pocket. "I wouldn't take nuffin for my striped ball," he said, and climbed upon his dismayed daddy's lap. Everybody laughed and I believe June was relieved as he tucked the bill of money back into his wallet. Everybody got their pop and cakes and the stories began.

Allen Hale got things started off by saying that the Crab Orchard school teacher, Mrs. Bond, told him that his boy, Roger had been coming late to school every day. Allen said Roger didn't like school and it was hard getting him started of a morning. Mrs. Bond said she finally told Roger he must get to school by the time she rang the bell each morning. The next morning, however, Roger was late again. So Mrs. Bond ask him, "Roger, why are you late again?" Roger said he heard that the school house was burned down. Mrs. Bond thought she had him there, so she said, "Well why did you come at all?" Roger looked her straight in the eye and without cracking a smile, said, "I didn't believe it."

After everyone got through saying, "Now that Roger is something else," and "No sir, you can't pull one over on ole Roger," June Mead looked over where the children were sitting and said, "I sure do remember my first day at school. I was scared to death. As a matter of fact, I was so nervous that morning that I cut my face all to pieces a-shaving." The children just loved that story. I wondered if it was true. But nobody ever asked story tellers if their stories were true. That would have been bad manners.

My daddy said that schools sure were different from when he was a boy. For one thing, everybody walked to school. They enjoyed it, although it made things a little tough when they started high school. From Possum Holler, it took several hours to walk back and forth to St. Paul High School, so Daddy rode his homemade bicycle. But finally, Mary Martin, the missionary to the Presbyterian churches, and Fred Hall on Dry Fork, and some others got together and gave money for a school bus to be built and run to St. Paul high school. Roy Cox, from Crab Orchard, had the bus special made and started driving it. There wasn't any charge to ride it, Daddy said, so it kept a lot of kids going to school beyond grade school. The kids who rode the bus called it Cox's army so Roy Cox painted that name on the side of it. It was the first school bus in Wise County.

Daddy said that while he was in about the fifth grade at Crab Orchard, the WPA came to school and dug out a level spot and told them it was to play basketball on. "Well," Daddy said, "We didn't know nothing about basketball. Baseball is all we knew anything about. So we looked it over and allowed we couldn't play no ball on that little bitty spot. They didn't give us a ball or put up a hoop, just dug out a little level spot.

"We wouldn't even a had a baseball except my dad found some old work socks, with holes in them, in a run-down house that some people had moved out of. Dad unraveled the socks and got a piece of clay and shaped it into a little round hard ball. Then we wrapped the yarn from the socks around the clay. We'd wrap and turn and wrap and turn. After we got the ball the right size, Mother took a needle and thread and sewed the outside so it wouldn't unravel." Somebody asked Daddy didn't they ever use the level spot the WPA dug. He said as a matter of fact they did shoot some marbles there sometimes. He said they played with p-jibs, crockies, and agates. Daddy said he started out with p-jibs which were marbles made from clay. Two p-jibs would get you one crocky which was a glazed p-jib. And you could trade five crockies for one agate. After they played marbles a while, Daddy won enough to trade for some nice crockies and agates.

Daddy said that a basketball team from a little school in Car Creek, Kentucky, that won state championship one year, had started the same way. The WPA had dug out a level spot on the top of a hill. But this time they put up a goal and gave them a basketball. They didn't know anything about uniforms, so they played in cut off blue jeans and won state championship. And a team from Flatgap High School did the same thing and when they won state championship by making about 90 percent of their shots from the floor, reporters come in there and wanted to know how they did it. Well, they said, they had to shoot good because, in practice, if one of them missed a shot, the ball rolled and bounced near a mile down the mountainside and whoever shot and missed had to go and fetch the ball back. Then too, they said, playing inside was so much easier than playing outside because you didn't have to figure on windage when you shot the ball on the inside. Everybody laughed about that but it sounded reasonable to me. Daddy said that once mountain boys got the hang of basketball they made mighty good players. "It was Glen Roberts from Pound that developed the jump shot," he said. "And the year he developed it, he set a scoring record that was never broken by the old rules. You see, back then, when a team scored, they walked back to center court and had a jump ball again. That was prior to 1937. Anyway, Glen walked five miles to Pound High School and five miles home and played basketball. He graduated in 1931 and his junior and senior years Pound won state championship both years. He went to Emory and Henry college and in 104 games scored 2013 points for a 19.4 per game average, which was a world record. Playing by the old rules, that kind of scoring was phenomenal. Emory and Henry played all larger schools, but still yet, in his four years, Glen made all conference, all state, and in his junior and senior years he was

All American. He was featured in Ripley's Believe it or Not, and every pro basketball team in the country wanted him to play for them. But Glen, he decided he'd rather come back to Wise County and teach and coach basketball. During the summers, however, Glen and his six brothers had their own team and traveled for Firestone Rubber Co. and played colleges and independent teams and beat them all. One of the reasons that Glen was so successful is that he used the jump shot and, since he was the one to develop it, no one knew how to guard against it. Of course, after the mountain boy developed it, everybody uses it."

Daddy said there was a Coleman boy in Eastern Kentucky that could play basketball about like Glen Roberts, but because of some family problems was unable to go to college and play. "In high school, though, he broke all scoring records, so it was a tragedy that he didn't get to go on like Glen did."

June Mead asked wasn't there some mountain boys that played baseball right well too. Daddy said that the Hillman boys from Scot County were excellent players because they could throw so well, growing up on a farm and all. "Darus Hillman (Dave we all called him) is the one everybody knows about, going professional and all. But his cousin, Winfield Hillman, was an even better pitcher than Dave. I've seen Winfield kill a deer on the first try with a rock about the size of a baseball, hit him right between the eyes and kill him dead. He learned to throw like that, a-keeping the rabbits out of the beans there on the farm. That man didn't need a gun to hunt with, he had such an arm. But when he went into the service, he got his shoulder injured, and after that, he couldn't throw but a few balls before his shoulder began to pain him something awful. But he'd of made an even better player than Dave if it hadn't a-been for his injury. And, of course, everybody has heard how well Tracy Stallard from Wise is doing. He's pitching major league too. Yes sir, mountain boys can sure play ball when they get the chance to."

Daddy said that the WPA was formed back when the government was trying to get everybody out of poverty. "They didn't send outsiders in here to build roads and basketball courts and other projects, they hired local people. Some of the people got to calling the government help 'relief.' One man, who lived back in the mountains was laid off from his WPA job. So the man's wife wrote a letter to Washington and complained that her husband had his project cut off and she hadn't had no relief since." Everybody laughed at that and I did too but I didn't really see the humor in it.

Grandpa Hall said that people used to say that WPA stood for "we pittle around." He said that Labourn Lawson saw a WPA worker lean on his shovel so long once, that the cut worms eat clean through the handle which broke off and nearly gouged a hole through the man.

Everybody got to talking about what a good meeting we had at church and about how the church caught on fire the night Sallings preached on hell. Uncle Maynard said his favorite preachers were Uncle Ben and Uncle Wade Powers. He said that Uncle Cleve Robinette was saved in one of Uncle Ben Power's meetings at Cherry Grove Freewill Baptist Chruch and Cleve had been the biggest moonshiner ever heard tell of. Cleve, himself, said that he guessed he had sold more moonshine than any other man alive. He wholesaled as well as retailed. Uncle Maynard said that after he was saved, Cleve testified at a Dan Graham tent meeting that he had made enough moonshine to float a battleship from Dwina to the Clinch River. Uncle Maynard said that Cleve himself made one of the finest preachers that ever lived after he was saved.

Grandpa Hall said that years ago, Orben Wells was one of the best liked preachers in the country. He said that one time the people in Virginia City got Orben to come hold a revival meeting but when he got to the church the coal company that built the church locked the door and wouldn't let him preach. Grandpa said that Orben told them that he come to preach and he didn't need a building to do it in. A man of God could preach anywhere. So Orben went down by the railroad and preached to the crowd that gathered to hear him. There were telegraph lines running along the railroad and somehow Orben's voice must have been picked up on them and transmitted over the radio. People heard him on their radios clear into Bluefield, West Virginia. Grandpa looked around the room to make sure everyone was getting the story, then added, "Now that's what can happen when they try to silence a man of God." It reminded me of the story of Daniel in the lion's den, it was so good.

"I was at the church when Orben preached his last sermon," Grandpa said. "He preached the Sunday morning service at Virginia city and it come an awful flood. After church, he carried James, there, to the car. I had a T-model ford at that time. We drove Orben to our house and then after dinner drove him to Crab Orchard to the Methodist Protestant Church where he preached his last service. When that service was over, we took him home with us for supper and then he walked across the mountain from Hall Holler to Bull Run, where he lived. That week he was in a mining accident at Pine, and that took his life. He was one of the finest preachers that ever walked these hills."

Allen Hale and Wallace Bond agreed that they liked to hear J.B. Quillen from Kingsport preach awful well. Daddy said that he liked Dan Graham better than any revival preacher he had ever heard. He said he guessed Dan Graham held more meetings and done as much to clean up the mountains as any man that ever lived. Daddy said that back in the early days, Dan would go in and set up his tent where there weren't any churches and when he preached, people laid down their guns and shut down their moonshine stills. I had heard Dan Graham preach. I liked to hear him because not only was he a bible scholar, he also was an expert on religion in general, world history, the economic situation, and politics. And he could explain everything so that a child could understand it because he used wonderful illustrations. I heard him tell one time how that the government was going deeper and deeper into debt. He talked about government programs, and waste, and the flagrant use of our resources. Then he said that it was like the billy goat that was shipped from the East coast to California by train. When the goat arrived in California, two men unloaded it and began looking for the shipping tag to see where to deliver it. Then one of them noticed that the goat was eating the tag. "We're in trouble now, he said, this goat has done eat where he's going." Dan Graham said that was just what America was doing. "If we don't stop our runaway spending and start conserving our resources," he said, "We'll be just like that goat, because we, too, are eating where we're going. In other words, we're spending and using up what rightfully belongs to our grandchildren and there will be nothing left for them if this trend continues." I'll never forget the impression that and other illustrations made on me. And I never knew anyone that loved poor people, black and white, the way Dan Graham did. He took a strong stand against sin because he knew how devastating and demoralizing it could be and had been for people. They said that Dan Graham was a logger before he was a preacher and he was not afraid to go right into some of the most lawless areas and preach.

Grandma Hall spoke up and said that the best loved old-time preacher in that country had to have been Preacher James Smith from Big Stone Gap. Smith was an old-time Presbyterian and he established an orphanage there in Big Stone and ran it all by himself. She said that one day when preacher Smith was walking down the street in town he came upon a man who was barefooted. That was during the depression, she said, and people was awful hard up. Preacher Smith looked around and there was nary a person in sight—he didn't want to do it for show—so he reached down and took the shoes off his own feet and handed them to the man. "But he gave the man more than shoes," Grandma said. "With that act of kindness, he give the man hope. About a week later, Smith went into the dry goods store there in Big Stone to get himself another pair of shoes but the owner said, 'No, you can't buy any shoes in my store. I saw what you done last week for that barefooted man out there on the street. Pick out the shoes you want, and they're yours—free of charge."

Grandma said another well-liked old-time preacher was

Uncle John Kennedy. He was a Freewill Baptist. He was holding a revival meeting on Dry Fork once and the meeting was almost broke up by drunks. (There was a still about a half mile up the holler.) Preacher Kennedy was about to quote Matthew 16:18 one night and had the still and the devil on his mind and so he misquoted the scripture. He said, "Upon this rock I will build my church, and Hell ain't a half mile from here."

June Mead said that he had always heard about what a big church-worker Uncle Terry Gibson was. Uncle Terry went to Bond Memorial in Crab Orchard and although he wasn't a preacher, he was real faithful in the church. He taught and led singing. Uncle Terry had heard his son, Sevier, say that he had gotten his hide dirty putting oil in the car. So he told Sevier never to say hide, to always say skin. One night when they were having a revival, Uncle Terry was leading the singing and the song was "Hide Me Oh My Savior Hide Me." So Sevier, being young and mischievous, decided that would be a good time to obey his dad's instructions, so he sung it, "Skin Me oh my Savior Skin Me."

Of course everyone agreed that the Gibsons were all wonderful church workers and good singers.

Finally, Leon Lawson picked up a coke bottle and blew on it and said, "James, let's sing some songs." Wallace Bond asked Leon how he found out that a coke bottle was in the key of b-flat. Leon said he didn't remember the first time somebody keyed up by a coke bottle. Uncle Maynard said it was probably Roscoe Reed that figured it out and Roscoe probably knew what key all the other bottles were in too. I remembered Roscoe. I had attended several of his singing schools. I learned to sing my do re me's about the same time I learned to use a spoon. Everybody in the mountains could look at a new song and sing it because we had singing schools at our churches every year. It was almost as important to read music as it was to read the Bible. My Grandma Hall told me that even when she was a little girl, a Mr. Heldrich went from church to church teaching people to sing. And Daddy said that when he was young, Willard Trent held singing schools at the Top of the Hill and elsewhere. But the man that taught more music than anyone else in the mountains was Roscoe Reed. Roscoe wrote gospel songs and had them published. Quartets all over the country sang them.

Leon had gone to his car and got some songbooks and everybody turned to page 132, "There Is A Fountain." Leon blew on the coke bottle again and we commenced to sing in four part harmony:

> *There is a fountain filled with blood*
> *Drawn from Immanuel's veins*
> *And sinners plunged beneath that flood*

Lose all their guilty stains.

E'er since by faith I saw the stream
Thy flowing wounds supply
Redeeming love has been my theme
And shall be till I die

Then in a nobler, sweeter song
I'll sing Thy pow'r to save
When this poor, lisping, stamm'ring tongue
Lies silent in the grave.

After that song, we sang Wallace Bond's favorite: "Oh that City on Mount Zion." And since Daddy didn't bring his pitch pipe, we sang them all in b-flat.

CHAPTER 10

WINDS OF CHANGE

Summer hit with a passion that year. Or maybe I hit summer with a passion. Either way it was a good one. Diana came in from Norfolk and my other cousins were getting old enough to be a lot of fun. Mother still worked at the factory in St. Paul, so Diana and I spent most of our days with one or the other of my grandmas. Mother liked working at the factory because she was real fast with her hands. So when she first started working, she made well over production. The company didn't like paying too much in wages, so when anyone made over production, they cut the pay scale and then the women had to work harder just to keep up with where they were before.

When Mother first went to work, they paid seven to eight cents a dozen to run lace across the back yoke of a slip. After a few months they paid just three to four cents a dozen. There wasn't anything that could be done about it either. If the women who had jobs complained, the company just hired someone else. And there were plenty of women wanting to work and the ones with jobs were the lucky ones. Mother said she didn't mind the hard work because she was able to put back a little money from each paycheck to pay for nurse's training one day. She clung to her dream. Daddy and I didn't like the way she had to work though. The machines were too loud. We were afraid she would go deaf. And the nylon dust filled the air so thick that Mother said the women could chew it. Some of the women had to quit because some machines were high and they had to stand on their feet all day. We didn't have to wonder how hot it was in the factory. When Mother came home, her dress was still ringing wet from the neck to the waist where she sweated in all the heat. The harder my mother worked, the more determined I was to get her a beautiful ring for her finger. I was saving every penny I could make. I was still washing canning jars and digging ginseng and gathering scrap metal with Daddy. I would never forget.

Now that Lucy and Shirley and I were older and associating with teenagers, our talk changed, and a disturbing issue was settling in among us. It suddenly became grown-up to discuss future plans. I hadn't ever thought about the future before. Now, all of a sudden, one of the older kids would look at me and say, "What you gonna do when you finish school?" I didn't know it was that important but I allowed I'd better start giving it some thought. I talked to Diana about it and she already knew she wanted to be a veterinarian. I could see that I had to say something and since Pansy and I wrote poetry together, I decided to say that I was giving some serious thought to being a writer.

74

That seemed to be a sufficient answer so I stuck with it.

I figured out what all the commotion was about. Clinch Valley College had opened in 1954 at Wise and a lot of parents wanted their children to get an education so they could get good jobs and not have to work in the coal mines. Clinch Valley was a branch of the University of Virginia and you could go there for two years. Boys could transfer to the University, and girls went somewhere else to finish. The building of that college was about the biggest thing that ever happened to the mountains, a lot of people said. But I heard some people laugh and say that them younguns that wanted to go to college was just trying to get above their raising. But anyway, that's why people started asking what you wanted to be when you grew up. Before Clinch Valley College, most people didn't have that choice. Diana and I asked Grandma Robinette about some people saying that kids would be getting above their raising, and she just hugged us both and said, "If going to college is getting above your raising, then I sure hope all my younguns get above their raising." I told Diana that we shouldn't talk in front of Pansy about college and what we wanted to be when we got out of school. I couldn't see any use in it. Anyway, I'd already decided that I was never going to do anything any different. I didn't like change.

I had seen what happened to some people who left the mountains. Marvin Taylor had quit school and gone off to Detroit and got a job working for Ford Motor company. Everybody said he made big money too. Every summer he came in for a week and drove around in his big Lincoln car. That's all he did—just drove around day and night and blew his car horn and waved at people. Sometimes he'd offer one of the girls a ride. But Mrs. Taylor told Mother that whenever it was time for Marvin to go back to Detroit, he sat down and cried like a baby.

It just didn't seem to me that a Lincoln car was worth all that. I'd rather stay in the mountains and drive a coal truck. But then, if Marvin didn't want to work in a coal mine, he didn't have much choice. Detroit, Akron, and Baltimore, that's where they all went. But as far as I could tell they all were just putting in time—living for the day they could come home to the mountains. Even my uncles who went to Norfolk and Detroit to work, talked about how much longer it would be before they could retire and come back to the mountains. They had good jobs and fine homes and cars, but they lived for the day they could come home again.

I looked into my pool to try to find the answer. They were all there—hundreds of years of wisdom staring back at me. But they stayed silent. I knew all I had to do was find the key because the answers were right there in my pool. And I'd unlock it one day.

Daddy's day off from work was Friday. And one Friday

morning in the middle of summer, Daddy borrowed Grandpa Hall's pickup truck and went to Coeburn. When he came back, he had a television and an antenna with him. The rest of the day, I stood in the front room and Diana stood in the doorway and we yelled, "good, worse, better, better, right there, hold it," while Daddy carried the antenna around the yard. By the time Mother got home from work, we were watching our own television. Diana and I liked cartoons and some of the commercials. Some of the westerns were pretty good but I would a whole lot rather have gone to the rock hole or to the Top of the Hill. I thought television would be real nice for Pansy though. I tried to tell her about the cartoons but it was too hard to describe them and I couldn't draw one lick.

One night, while we were watching television, we saw a large swimming pool and a diving board. Diana and I got after Daddy to fix us one of those at the rock hole. And Daddy did. He took a long two by ten down to the river and fastened it on to the tall flat rock out in the deep part of the rock hole. The board was springy and every time someone tried to dive off, they flipped over—sometimes two or three times before they hit the water. I enjoyed the diving board so much that sometimes during church it was all I could do to keep my mind on the preaching because I knew we would be going to the river right after the service to picnic and swim and dive.

When Diana and I went to church with our Grandma and Grandpa Robinette, it wasn't hard to keep my mind on the preaching. Covy Robinette was the Free Will Baptist preacher at that time and he preached about sin and death and the judgement day and the wrath of God and the importance of being saved. And he preached it loud enough so I didn't have to try to listen. It got through whether I listened or not. I liked it though. I figured that between the Presbyterians and the Free Wills, I got it all. At my church, I learned the catechism, the creeds, the importance of the communion service, tithing, the sovereignty of God, and the importance of being saved. Being saved was one thing they all agreed on. At the end of the service at the Free Will Baptist church, we usually stood in a circle and held hands and sang "Will the Circle Be Unbroken."[1]

> *Will the circle be unbroken*
> *By and by, Lord, by and by*
> *There's a better home a-waiting*
> *In the sky, Lord, in the sky.*

But that summer the circle was broken, when several miners from over on Bull Run were killed in a mining accident.

1. Reprinted by permission of the publisher, R.E. Winsett Music Co.

I thought they should just close down all the mines until they could make them safe. Daddy said the mines were a lot better than they used to be. He said that when his Daddy got back from World War I and Walter Reed Hospital and went to work in a coal mine in Holden, West Virginia, the miners had to furnish their own tools. He said the tools cost a lot too. They had to furnish the pick and shovel and breastplate and auger and needle. They also had to provide their own axe and tamping bar and carbide lamp and carbide. And they even had to provide the powder and paper and make their own cartridges. That was before they had dynamite. If the mine had water in it, the miners had to buy their own gum rubber boots. And if the water was too deep they had to dip it out before they could start shooting and digging and loading. He said most mines back then had water and the miners got eat up with rheumatism. Grandma Hall always kept pokeberry wine because it was the only thing that would cure the rheumatism. The miners worked six days a week from before daylight to way after dark and they said the only time in their whole lives they ever saw their children in the daylight was Sunday.

Daddy said that a miner couldn't complain about the working conditions or the boss man would just say there was a line of barefoot men a-waiting for his job. "Yeah," Daddy said, "They came in here and paid almost nothing for the mineral rights to this land to people who had no earthly way of knowing what it would mean to them and the mountains. And then they put the same men to work as little more than slaves in holes underneath the very land they once owned and cherished. And when the coal companies got all the coal they could from one mine they pulled out and started in on another spot, leaving running sores all over the mountains."

I almost wished I hadn't brought up the subject of coal mines. But now, at least, anytime I wanted to get my mind off everything, I could watch television. Daddy liked to watch boxing and some of the funny programs. We usually put potatoes in the ashes of the stove or popped popcorn and sat down in front of the set two or three times a week. But distressing thoughts began to plague my mind. I noticed that a lot of the funny shows had tall gawky men who acted lazy and stupid. They were dressed in overalls with one of the galluses hanging down. They wore holey hats and went barefooted. But the worst part of it was they all called each other cousin—I mean the husbands and wives were cousins too. That's probably why they were acting like idiots. Everybody laughed. But I noticed something else. The people on those shows were called "hillbillies." What upset me the most was that they depicted hillbillies as lazy and dimwitted. Everybody I knew in Wise and the surrounding counties and everybody I'd heard about who lived years earlier had been industrious. Actually, mountain people often wound up crippled or dead, men and women both, because of all the rough and dangerous work they did. I knew miners who, right then, were doubling back and working two shifts in low coal. That type of work would have already killed the average man. And it was their quick wit and way with words and stories that had entertained and thrilled me since I was a kid. I asked Diana if she thought the television programs were trying to poke fun at us, but she said she believed they were mocking someone else in another part of the country— Colorado perhaps.

I was glad, then, that Pansy didn't have a television. I was sure she would notice right off how they were depicting hillbillies. I figured she was a lot better off reading books. And anyway, at the beginning of summer the school teacher had given her ten books to read, including Moby Dick. I decided not to talk to her about television any more. We laughed at ourselves all the time at the Top of the Hill. And that was all right. But those poor, lazy people on television weren't funny. They were pathetic.

Not only did we get a television that summer, we got a telephone and a telephone book too. Anytime Diana and I didn't have anything else to do, we'd ease up the receiver and listen in to the conversation on the line. One day we decided to play a joke on my uncle Victor. We looked up the number of Estes Funeral Home in Coeburn and watched for Uncle Victor to get in from his job at the prison camp in Flat Woods. Then I changed my voice and called and told him that someone from that number had a box for him and he was to call and ask for it. We gave him time to dial the number, then we picked up the phone and listened in. Even though they answered "Estes Funeral Home," Uncle Victor asked them if they had a box for him. After a lot of confusion and talk about Uncle Victor's box, the people at the funeral home finally told him that he had called the funeral home and that someone must have played a prank. It's the first time I ever heard Uncle Victor curse. Diana and I sat straight faced that night and shook our heads and clicked our tongues against our teeth while we listened to him tell about some "fool" having him call the funeral home and ask for his box. Later, we laughed about it all night.

CHAPTER 11

STORYTELLING IN THE RAIN

We kept swimming and playing and going to Pansy's house and reading with her, but it sure was a summer that lay heavy on my mind. When Uncle Ralph and Aunt Grace came to get Diana, we went to the Top of the Hill one night, and Uncle Ralph and Aunt Grace got to be there too. It was raining and the beating of rain on a tin roof makes you even hungrier for tall tales.

After everybody got their pop and cakes, Daddy got the stories started with Uncle Dan Ramey. "Back when Uncle Dan was living they didn't have too good a law enforcement and ever so often there were killings and the like. Well, a Sultzer man from Scott County rode up to the Flat Woods about every week. Now I don't rightly know what his business was in Wise County but the people over in the Flat Woods begin to fear him or take a great disliken to the man somehow. Well, one evening Uncle Dan was a-riding through the Flat Woods when he come upon Sultzer's horse laying beside the road, dead. Uncle Dan jumped down off of his horse and looked around and could see blood splattered all over a rock and a pool of blood on the ground around the rock. Well, Uncle Dan took a rock and beat the shoes off the horse.

"Back then times were hard, it was root hog or die. Horseshoes were hard to come by and there certainly wasn't any use wasting some on a dead horse. Then he saw the saddle stuck up in a holler tree. And on the ground beside the horse was Sultzer's pipe, still smoking. Uncle Dan bent over to pick up the pipe but everytime he touched it he said that something went 'zip, zip' around his head. That scared Uncle Dan so he threw down the pipe and headed for Guest's Station. Guest's Station, you know, was the name for Coeburn at that time. Anyway, the river was up and roaring and there wasn't any bridge across it. When Uncle Dan reached Guest's Station, he told them exactly what he'd seen. Well, they noticed that he wasn't at all wet and somebody said, 'Dan, how'd you get across Guest's River?' Uncle Dan studied it over a while and then said, 'Begod, I didn't cross Guest's River.' Of course he had to have crossed the river to get to Coeburn from Flat Woods.

"When the men got back out to the Flat Woods, they found everything just like Uncle Dan had told it. And the blood is on that rock to this day."

The rain was hitting the tin roof. I leaned back in my chair and propped my feet on the stove—I could do it now without falling—and I wished that God would stop time and let us stay here forever eating our moon pies and drinking our pop with the little ice crystals inside and listening to the rain and the stories.

About that time, lightning struck up on the hill behind the store and several people jumped. Uncle Ralph said that it was getting a little close for comfort. Then everybody that was near the windows scooted in toward the middle of the room a little. Daddy said that people used to think that feathers protected them against lightning. "One time Ma lived next to Uncle Dan and Aunt Dice. Ma was over visiting with Dice when it came up a thunderstorm. Back then, people thought that if you were covered with feathers, lightening couldn't strike you, so Dice, she headed for the featherbed and crawled in under it, but Ma paced. She walked from the front door to the back a-watching the storm. Ever now and then Dice poked her head out from under the feather bed and said, 'Pray Catherine pray.' And then she'd say, 'Is the storm getting any better?'

" 'No,' Ma would say, 'It's worse than ever, the trees are a thrashing and breaking all around the house.'

"Well, after a little while, Dice poked her head out again and hollered, 'Pray, Catherine, Pray.'

" 'Dice,' Ma said still pacing, 'the Bible says to watch as well as pray.' "

That was the first time I ever heard a story on Uncle Dan's wife. I wondered where they got the idea that feathers would protect them from lightening. I figured they thought that's what protected the birds. Daddy said that one time Uncle Dan come to visit his grandpa, (Uncle Johnny Hall). Uncle Johnny and Rosa were gone delivering milk and eggs but his Daddy, Oscar, and Oscar's half sister, Aunt Bertha were at home so Uncle Dan decided to wait for Uncle Johnny's return. "It come up an awful thunder storm with lightning striking the hillside just every minute or two. Aunt Bertha was just a young girl and she saw that Uncle Dan was afraid of the storm so she slipped out onto the porch and got the water bucket. After a while she threw the water bucket against the wall behind Uncle Dan and he thought he'd been struck by lightening. He let out a yell and jumped clean across the room and fell down and grabbed his heart like he was dying. Of course, Dad and Aunt Bertha were laughing like a couple of hyenas and when Uncle Dan realized what had happened, it embarrassed the daylights out of him. So he stood up, turned to Dad and said, 'I've hyeard all my life that the Halls are a bunch of dam fools and there (pointing to Aunt Bertha) stands a full-bloodied one.' "

Daddy said the only other time he ever heard of Uncle Dan getting scared of anything, was when he decided to ride the train from Coeburn to Virginia City. "Back then people went to Coeburn and rode the train to its next stop just to see what it was like. Well, Uncle Dan boarded and took a seat but he got afraid to look out the window because they were moving so fast.

Finally he thought he'd risk one peek, but just as he looked, they were crossing the Lawson trestle over at Bull Run and Uncle Dan thought they'd gone airborne—he had heard about airplanes so he believed he was flying. He slapped both hands over his eyes and kept them covered until they pulled into Virginia City. The conductor come through just as the train stopped, so Uncle Dan turned to him and yelled, 'Has she lit?' "

After everyone stopped laughing, Daddy said, "Now I want you all to know the story of the Dan Ramey Bear Cliff because the National Forest Service come in here and named it Bear Rock and everybody is going to forget where it got its name. Uncle Dan used to sell anything he could get his hands on. People did back then. They dug gensing and mayapple and they fished and hunted for game and bee trees and nuts and berries and chinquapins and greens and what they couldn't use, they sold or traded. The rest they used and shared with neighbors. That's how they survived. Well anyway, Dan walked up little Stoney Creek where Little Stoney forks with Laurel Fork and a high cliff juts out above there. Uncle Dan climbed upon that cliff and there he caught himself two cub bears. Well, he put one under each arm and headed back down Little Stoney Creek for Dungannon. In Dungannon, he sold the bears to a traveling salesman who said he could sell them to a circus. Some of the people wanted to know where he caught the cubs, and they were able to backtrack him all the way to the cliff by the pieces of clothing and the beard and the blood torn from him by them two bear cubs. They tracked him to the very rock where he caught them. Now that's how come it's called the Dan Ramey Bear Cliff. They shouldn't call it Bear Rock or people will forget."

I believe we all loved Uncle Dan stories because he represented for us the big fearless Scotch-Irish that settled our land.

But Daddy was just getting started good. I think he liked story-telling in the rain. So he didn't slow down. He said, "One time Dan was telling about a deer he had seen. He said it was back on the High Knob and the trees were so thick you couldn't get a knife between them and he said the deer had a rack of horns four feet wide. Somebody asked Uncle Dan how the deer managed to get between the trees with a rack of horns that wide. 'Begod,' said Dan, 'That's the deer's business, not mine.' "

Without so much as waiting for everyone to stop laughing, Daddy launched into the fishing story. "Uncle Dan was fishing in Guest's River once when some men came by with a big string of fish they had caught. Uncle Dan hadn't caught but a few fish and he looked at his string and looked at theirs and said, 'Begod, wonder how it would look with all the fish on one string.' Then he took their fish and put them on the string with his and held them up and looked at them and said, 'Begod, now ain't that a

81

beautiful sight.' Then he picked up his fishing pole and said, 'Well, boys, let's go to Guest's Station.' and Uncle Dan walked on down the railroad with everbody's fish. He left the men standing with nothing but their mouths dropped open. That's why you hear people say, 'Wonder how they'd all look on one string.' Yeah, that's how that saying got started."

Daddy cleared his throat and kept going. "One time Uncle Dan's turkeys got out and he commenced looking for them. Finally he found them out on the far end of Sandy Ridge, walking along scratching in the dirt and leaves. Uncle Dan said that as he approached, one of the turkeys said 'put,' and they put all right. they put clean up on the High Knob. Uncle Dan never did see his turkeys again."

Uncle Ralph said that mountain men could live by their wits when they took a notion to. He said that a couple of the Bond boys wanted to travel around and see the country—see what it was like outside the mountains, so they saved some money and set out hitchhiking. But they ran out of money before they ran out of trip and decided they'd have to get a place to sleep and food to eat for a few days and maybe a little cash. It was on a Saturday night and they saw people gathering for a church service. They went in and introduced themselves as traveling evangelists and wanted to know if they could hold a revival meeting for the people. Everybody thought that was wonderful and that they must have been sent from God. The Bond boys were good singers, and being brought up in church, they knew how to preach. And they preached and sang for three nights to large crowds. They were so good at it, in fact, that people were saved almost nightly. The preacher had insisted they stay with him and his family but he was one that believed that a little wine at bed time was good for the body so he kept a gallon jug under his bed and took a little nip each night. The preacher offered the Bond boys a little drink, and they wanted to drink some of it but they also wanted to sound pious so they told the preacher that they wouldn't mind a little drink "if it weren't intoxicating." After three nights of a little drink from that jug, the boys couldn't stand it any longer, they just had to have more. So the next night after the preacher had his drink and went to bed they gathered their clothes together and the cash they had collected at the meetings and slipped off their shoes and snuck into the preacher's bedroom and stole his jug and hightailed it out of there. Uncle Ralph said they were still laughing about it when they got home.

Uncle Victor said that one of the Holbrook boys got it in his mind one time to travel around and see the country cause he had got him a car. "It was back during the depression and they were rationing gasoline. So Harless, he rigged up an extra gas tank in his car and got him a bottle and filled it full of all the little pills he could find. Then he lit out. He didn't have any money and he needed some right away so as soon as he got out of the mountains—you know he had to wait until he was out of the mountains cause he couldn't a fooled nobody around here with that. As soon as he got out of the mountains, he stopped at a service station where there were several men standing around and he asked if he could get some water. The station owner showed him where the water was and Harless got a bucket and got the water. Then he poured the water into his fake tank and taken that pill bottle out of his pocket and dropped a pill in the tank and got in his car and headed down the road right slow. Sure enough, the men from the service station overtook him and wanted to know what he'd take for some of them pills. He told them he didn't have too many but he reckoned he would sell a few. He did that all over the country back during the depression. Made a good living at it too."

We loved stories like that so Daddy said, "Lloyd Hall was left an orphan and got started hoboing around the country when he was right young. He went into a restaurant one day and asked if they would take a man's last penny for a meal. They told him they sure would. He ordered one of the best meals on the menu and after he ate his fill, walked up to the cash register and said here it is and lay down a penny. They called the manager who finally decided that they had agreed to take the penny before he ordered. He got himself a good meal for one cent."

We were all into the stories in a big way by now and everybody was laughing and the story-tellers were talking louder to talk over the storm and Diana and I poked each other and laughed and watched the men slap their knees and talk about what a good one that was. Then Uncle Ralph said that it was the Scotch-Irish who got the storytelling started in this country. "The English never did have much of a sense of humor," he said. He told how that one time an Englishman was passing through the mountains and stopped in at a little store and heard someone say, "We eat what we can, and what we can't, we can." Everybody laughed, and so the Englishman thought it must have been funny and he thought that when he got back to England he'd tell it. But when he retold the story, he said, "In America they have a saying: We eat what we can, and what we can't, we tin." Uncle Ralph said that of course no one laughed and the Englishman couldn't figure out why they didn't.

Daddy said that right after he went to work for Watt's Produce, tomatoes got right scarce. He was in a store in Kentucky and he was explaining to the owner about it and he told the owner that Canada had plenty of tomatoes and they could get them from there but the tariff eats them up. One of the men standing in the store studied about it for a minute and said, "You know, I'll bet that's what got on mine and eat them

83

up."

On another occasion, Daddy said, he was explaining to a merchant that the bottom had dropped out from under corn and it wasn't bringing anything. An old timer standing by the counter, said, "'sthat right? Why, I'm still getting $5 a gallon outa mine."

When Daddy first started at Watts Produce, there was another man working there by the name of Wolfe. Mr. Wolfe told Daddy that over in Kentucky one day he saw a sign that said, "Men Working 15 mile per hour." "And I'll be danged if I could see where they was working over five," he said.

Daddy said ever so often Mr. Wolfe would break into the same song:

> Oh the thousand legged worm
> He said as he did squirm
> Hasn't anybody seen a leg of mine
> If it can't be found
> Then I'll have to hop around
> On the other nine hundred ninty nine.

Wolfe told Daddy that when he was a young man, there had been an awful drought. The church people decided to call a special meeting and pray for rain. "And I'll be danged, if I wasn't the only one that showed up with an umbrella," he said.

Then Daddy told the match story: "There was a man who owned a store over in Dickenson County and one day a salesman come through a-selling matches. He was selling them by drop shipment. Now matches sell by the gross, you see. So the salesman told the owner that if he bought one gross, his profit would be about fifty cents. If he bought ten gross, his profit would be five dollars but if he bought a hundred gross his profit would be so enormous he could just sell the store and retire for life. Well, the store owner said he'd take the ones that made him the most profit. A couple of years later the match salesman went to selling brooms and come by the same store and over in one corner of the store was all them cases of matches stacked up high as your head. So the salesman said to the owner, 'My, you must be an awful good match salesman.' Now the owner didn't recognize him cause he was selling brooms this time. So the owner said 'No, I ain't a good match salesman at all, but the man that sold them matches to me is one hell of a good salesman."

Then Daddy asked us kids if we had heard about the old mountain man asking a young farmer if he raised any poultry. We said we hadn't heard that one, so he said the young man replied no, he had planted some poultry once, but the chickens scratched it all up.

About that time Uncle Victor said, "Reckon where ol

Labourn is tonight?" Bob Davis said that Labourn was under the weather and didn't feel like getting out. Wallace Bond asked if Labourn ever took anybody to see his village of little people that he used to talk about. Uncle Victor said that whenever anybody mentioned going, it was always the wrong time or cloudy or something. "Anyway," Uncle Victor said, "Labourn said that you could only see them one day out of the year and you had to be standing at exactly the right spot on the top of Osborne Ridge a-looking down into a valley. It had to be at precisely the right moment, and then you could watch them for only a few minutes because the sun had to be hitting it just right. Labourn said they were about two- to three-feet tall and had a whole little village built, church and everything. But Labourn ain't talked as much about it lately as he used to."

Then Uncle Maynard wanted to know if anybody knew how Clark Cassell was. Clark wasn't there either. Everybody said that Clark was doing fine but they didn't know why he wasn't there. He never was known to miss a night at the Top of the Hill. June Mead said that he believed Clark's knee from that old injury was bothering him again.

"What old injury is that?" Uncle Ralph asked.

"Well," June said, "You know Clark used to dig wells for people. He was digging one over in the Possum Holler one time and dug it so crooked, he plumb fell out of it. Ever since then he's had trouble with his knee every time it rains."

Daddy said maybe Clark was like the man that went to the doctor and said, "Doctor, I never felt better in my life." "Well," said the doctor, "why'd you come to me?" The man looked right at the doctor and said, "I thought it was about time I did."

It was that kind of night. They couldn't get serious about anything. I got another Grapette and a bag of peanuts. Then I poured the peanuts down into the Grapette. I had watched my little cousin, Jimmy, do that and it looked so good that I thought I'd give it a try. Diana got a SunKist. She pointed to the sign over the pop cooler that read, "Get kist for a nickle." We giggled and propped our feet on the stove again. When we settled back down, Edgar Davis began. "You all talk about smart men. One of the smartest men that ever lived is that Ed Ingle. Anybody that can build a radio station the way he did is a genius." Uncle Ralph hadn't heard about the radio station so he asked what radio station Ed built. "Well," said Edgar, "He got to looking at his radio one day. Now, Ed didn't get much of a formal education, he is self-taught. But he figured out how the radio worked by just taking it apart and studying it. Then he reckoned that if he reversed the process, he could transmit with it instead of receive. So he reversed it and with the help of some parts from the junkyard, he made himself a radio station."

"Does it work?" Uncle Ralph wanted to know. Of course, all

of us but Uncle Ralph knew that it worked because every Sunday when we got back from the rock hole, we turned on our radios and listened to Ed's station. After we got telephones in Possum Holler, we started calling in requests and everything. Some People clear over in Flat Woods had picked up his radio station. Edgar went on, "I've always said that if they ever want to put a man on the moon, they should send Ed Ingle, cause all they'd have to do is get him there. He'd figure out a way to get back."

Grandpa Hall said that another smart man was that Doc Livesay. "He doctors with herbs, you know. He's cured more people than any doctor in this country." Grandma said that he even cured cancer on people. She said she knew people he'd cured cancer on and that was after the medical doctors had give up on them. About everybody knew someone that Doc Livesay had cured with his herbs and potions. Grandma said that he cured her neighbor of cancer. "You could smell the sulfur in the stuff he put on her neck, but besides that we didn't know what else was in it. But when he came to take the bandage off the woman's neck, all of the cancer came with it and it had big long roots attached. But it all came out. It left a scar on her neck, but she lived for years and never had any more cancer."

I believe that's about all the talk about cancer anybody wanted, so for a little while everybody was quiet, trying to think how to change the subject and finally Daddy said, "Most of you all knew Claude Johnson." I could tell by the way everybody nodded and smiled that Claude must have been a real character. Daddy said, "Claude could throw his voice. I know they say that ventriloquists just seem to throw their voices, but Claude really could."

Edgar said, "I know that he could, I've stood right beside him when he would throw a ball up into a tree. He'd talk back and forth with someone. 'Catch it,' he'd say. Then the voice from up in the tree would say, 'I got it. Here it comes back down to you.' You'd swear there was someone in the top of that tree. The voice came down out of the top."

Uncle Ralph said that he once saw Claude stand beside a man who owned a T-model Ford. Claude made a noise just exactly like the T-Model firing up, and it scared the man because he thought his Ford was taking off without him and he ran and jumped in it.

"The best one he ever pulled," Daddy said, "was when he went over to Mann, West Virginia, to get a job. It was high coal and they could use a mule in the mine. Claude asked the bossman about a job and the boss told Claude he didn't need anyone right then; he had all the men he could use. Well, Claude slipped into the mine and watched the operation for a while. He saw that when the driver loaded the car and the mule started out, there was one right steep grade that the mule balked at every time and the driver would have to keep telling the mule to come up. So Claude, he hid behind a timber right near that steep grade and the mule driver loaded the car and started out with the coal. Mules do the same thing every time, so when the mule got to the steep grade, he balked on the driver again. When a mule won't go and you holler at him, he will nearly always turn his head and look over his shoulder at you. So the mule stopped and the driver hollered, 'Come up there.' The old mule didn't move, he just looked around at the man. Just as the mule looked around, Claude throwed his voice and said, 'Can't do it boss, load too heavy.' The driver looked at the mule and just couldn't believe his ears, so he hollered again, 'Come up there.' 'Can't do it boss,' said the mule, 'load too heavy.' At that, the driver throwed down the reins and took out of the mine a-flying. The bossman asked the driver what the trouble was. 'That mule has done started talking,' the man said.

"The bossman had a big laugh at that and said, 'Let's go back in and you show me this talking mule.' The boss was a crippled man and walked with a cane. But they went back to where the mule stood with the load of coal and the driver took the reins and said, 'Come up there.' The mule looked over his shoulder, and Claude throwed his voice again and the mule said, 'Can't do it boss, load too heavy.' That time they both ran from the mine but the bossman threw down his cane and outran the driver."

By the time Daddy got to the end everybody was dying laughing. "Anyway," Daddy said, "Claude got the job because the driver wouldn't go back into the mine anymore. But later, Claude got to laughing about what he had done and told the boss and the boss fired him for it, on the spot."

Uncle Ralph said that Claude Johnson was the only man he ever knew that could do five different things at one time. Daddy said he had seen him do it too and Wallace and Helen Bond said they had seen him do it a lot. Claude was Helen's uncle. Uncle Ralph said that you could give Claude four pieces of paper and four pencils and he'd write four different letters to four different people, two with his hands and two with his feet, and sing a song all at the same time.

Edgar Davis said that when Claude moved his family to Baltimore, he went up to visit a cousin, and while he was there his cousin took him out to where Claude worked. While Edgar and Claude were talking, Edgar asked Claude's boss if he'd ever seen Claude write four letters and sing a song all at the same time. The boss wouldn't believe that a man could do that so he went and got four pencils and four pieces of paper and said prove it. Claude obliged the boss without any trouble but Edgar said that the boss just got mad and said, "Well, a man as smart as you, should be doing five times the work that you are." Edgar said Claude looked at him and said, "Uh oh, Edgar, you've ruined me now."

Uncle Ralph said that Claude played the guitar and sang and he made up his songs as he went along. He said the man never had any trouble with words. Daddy said Claude had made up a song one time about the democrats a-going to the graveyard and voting the dead at election time and he named the names of the politicians that did it. Daddy said that Claude almost got in trouble over that one. Wallace said Claude was a good man and brilliant, but like everyone else in the mountains, it didn't do him much good. His family was always poor. Helen said that after Claude moved his family to Baltimore, though, they did right well.

Daddy said that Uncle Ed Wilson was certainly a man of many talents too. "He came in here with a crew to build the Swede Tunnel down on the railroad. After the tunnel was built he stayed and all he ever told anybody about his life was that he was from Ireland. He married Prudence Robinette (Grandpa Robinette's sister) and she already had two children because she had been married to Jim Hall. But one day Jim just up and disappeared. Anyway, Uncle Ed was a pianist, an artist, and a finish carpenter. Whenever somebody wanted something fancy built, they called on him. He's the one who built and painted the big hand-carved wall plaque out at the church." I loved that plaque, you could see it as soon as you walked in the church house. It was shaped like a scroll and the lettering was exquisite: "This church stands for loyalty to Christ, strict adherence to the Sabbath, and Christian loving and Christian living."

Grandpa Hall said that a lot of local men, including himself, helped build the Swede Tunnel. "They brought cement in there in cotton sacks. And when they used the cement, the workers were allowed to take the empty sacks home. You could wash them up and hem them and they made good towels that wouldn't ever wear out. As a matter of fact, we're still using some of them at our house."

Uncle Victor said he wanted to tell what happened to him last week-end. He said that he was up at his cabin on the High Knob when a car with out-of-state tags pulled up and stopped. Uncle Victor was superintendent of the state prison camp in the Flat Woods and he liked to get away and rest on week-ends sometimes, so he built his family that cabin on High Knob. Anyway, Uncle Victor said he was setting on his front porch—whittling when the car pulled up and a man in the drivers seat rolled down his car window and said, Hey Buddy, can you tell me where I can find some real hillbillies. Uncle Victor said he told the man, "Well stranger, this is your lucky day. You're looking at a real hillbilly if they ever was one." Well, Uncle

Victor carried on so and hollered for his wife to poke her head out so the strangers could see her too. Then he invited them in for some possum pie and told them to hang around cause the younguns was fetching a fresh jug up from the holler. And he told them that if they'd stick around they might even get to see some dead revenuers because he'd seen some sneaking around. Then Uncle Victor looked sorta sideways at the man in the car and said, "Say, you wouldn't happen to be one of them low-down sneakin' varmints, would you, cause if'n you are," But before Uncle Victor could finish, the man rolled up his window and took off down the road like a scared haint. Everybody was laughing at the things Uncle Victor said. But I knew why those people drove down to see some real hillbillies; And I expected there would be more to follow.

The storm had died down and Uncle Ralph said they'd better be getting on back down to Grandma Robinette's, because they would be leaving early in the morning. Mother asked Uncle Ralph and Aunt Grace to sing "Rainbow at Midnight"[1] before they left. Uncle Ralph got his guitar out of the car and they sang. Of course that song got most everybody to crying because it talked about a soldier coming back from the war.

> *After the war was over*
> *I was coming home to you*
> *I saw a rainbow at midnight*
> *Out on the ocean blue.*

Everybody knew that Uncle Ralph almost didn't make it home from World War II because he was a prisoner of war in a German Stalag. He had kept a diary while he was in there and people everywhere borrowed it and read it. Conditions were awful and a lot of men starved to death. The ones who lived ate whatever they could catch, including rats. The only food served them by the Germans was cabbage soup. Once, the men caught the guard dog and ate him. When the Germans demanded that the man who killed the dog step forward, every man there stepped forward. Uncle Ralph also said that a lot of men were taken from camp and never returned. They were real sick and "dropping like flies." But the prisoners did things that, in a strange way, kept their morale up. When German soldiers approached, the prisoners would say, "Hile de Fuhrer—de fewer de better." The Germans never caught on. When Uncle Ralph finally returned home, Grandma Robinette cooked a grand meal and had the whole family in for a celebration and thanksgiving.

---

1. Rainbow At Midnight, Words and Music by "Lost" John Miller Copyright (c) 1946 Shapiro, Bernstein & Co., Inc., New York. Copyright Renewed. International Copyright Secured. All Rights Reserved. Used by permission.

But when she put the cooked cabbage on the table, Uncle Ralph went straight outside and vomited. Of course, Grandma didn't know then about the cabbage soup. All of Grandma's sons went to fight in that war, but Uncle Ralph was the only one to get captured.

After Uncle Ralph's and Aunt Grace's song, everybody told them bye and hoped they had a safe trip back. I sure would like to have had Diana full time, instead of just for the summers.

CHAPTER 12

A BITTER BIOGRAPHY

I had a week before school started and I talked things over with Pansy—things I hadn't meant to tell her. But I knew it was something that would have to be settled sooner or later. Pansy knew about Clinch Valley college. I told her that even if I did go to college, I wouldn't leave the mountains. I'd stay right there and get a job at the sewing factory in St. Paul and every evening I'd come by and we'd read and write poems together. Pansy sat and patted her head with her finger as I was talking to her. When I finished she smiled and I smiled but she smiled with her mouth closed and that was unnatural and she didn't say it seemed like the right thing to do. It gnawed at my mind.

Pansy knew about the Scotch-Irish. She had read in a book where the first Declaration of Independence was drawn up by mountain men in Abingdon. So she didn't worry about television depicting mountain people as stupid or lazy. And she knew about our language and how it was Anglo Saxon and it was something to be proud of. She had said we should write some poetry and that would help us feel better about it. She was trying to write like Emily Dickinson. We wrote several poems and I felt a lot better about everything. Pansy was keeping all of our poetry in a book. We decided we would publish it one day when we got enough. Pansy wanted to call it, "Mayhem, Mirth and Miscellaney." It seemed like she was happiest when she was writing.

I went from Crab Orchard grade school to Coeburn high school that year and I never saw so many people in one school. I had three different teachers. One day our English teacher said she wanted us to write something in class. I figured it would be about how we spent our summers. I pretty much knew what I would write. But she said to write an autobiography. "Do any of you have any idea who you are? Do you know anything about your ancestry or heritage?" she said. "Tell me what it's like to be from the Appalachian Mountains. But make it brief—as few sentences as possible."

I was still a little bitter about those television shows. So instead of writing something nice, I got downright sarcastic and I certainly kept it short—I wrote one sentence: "Appalachia is not a place I like to talk about since it is dirty and poor and its natives are stupid and no one likes to admit being born here, but if you must know, you'll find that I come from a long line of Appalachian Saxons and all of the low life inbreeding possibly accounts for my damned double digit IQ."

Two days later, the teacher asked to see me during lunch. I

actually thought she might want to commend me on my writing style. Instead, she said she had never seen such a disgusting autobiography in all of her born days of teaching and that if I didn't write something good, she would call my parents. I wouldn't have minded her calling my parents except that I had used a curse word at the very end—only because it seemed to fit. But I didn't want any trouble. I wrote another autobiography. I got an A. I knew what she wanted.

Things improved fast at the high school, mainly because I developed a reputation for being good at sports. I joined the girl's softball team and my coach, Rex Paine, said I was the first person he ever saw that could hit a ball and then run all the bases before the ball ever touched the ground. The high schools also had powder-puff football teams that played flag football. I joined that too. Everytime I carried the ball, I ran a touchdown. Mother and Daddy brought Pansy to some of the games. She enjoyed cheering for me. But Pansy knew, and I knew why I could run so fast.

Then just after Christmas, the school announced try-outs for the annual 3-act play. I brought a playbook home and Mother helped me practice one of the parts. Finally, when the big night arrived, mother drove me to the school and waited outside in the Jeep. I walked into the gymnasium and sat down on the bleachers near the back and contemplated just leaving. It was mostly 11th and 12th graders there and they were milling around up front talking and laughing. I felt plumb out of place. I got up to slip out the door but then I saw them—the faces in my pool, hardened and focused—a perserverance kindled by undying faith, Grandma Robinette called it. Then I heard Grandpa Mullins say, "pon my word and honor child, don't never give up nor quit." And before I knew what was happening, I was up front, and Mrs. Johnson, the Latin teacher who helped with plays, was saying, "Oh Geraldine, I'm glad you came, you'll be reader 20."

I watched as one by one the other students read parts from the play. Some of them were good and some shook so hard they dropped things. Then it was my turn. I could feel my heart beating out of my chest and I looked down to see if it was noticeable. I walked out to the center of the stage, and suddenly, I was at home. I was back at the Top of the Hill church acting in the Christmas play or saying Bible verses or singing a song, as I had done many times before. I had memorized some of the lines of Aunt Harry Hornhonker and I said them with all the expression I could muster. The piece was funny, and before I was through, Mrs. Hilton and Mr. Shelburne, another teacher who helped direct the plays, laughed till they cried. I couldn't believe it. I got a part in Coeburn High School's play, "A Feudin Over Yonder." It certainly made me think about the difference a year can make in a person's life. I had Mother stop by Pansy's house on the way home so I could tell her the good news. Pansy and I decided life was like a path, it may be a little rocky and steep for a time, but around the next bend, it always changes. Pansy said it was like a Buckeye—half sweet, half poison—the key is in knowing which half to bite into. We decided to write several poems on the subject.

There was one strange thing about our school play. It occurred to me that we were playing the parts of hillbillies. But we were acting like and using the language of the characters we'd watched on television, who were doing a bad imitation of us in the first place. I tried not to think about it and just have fun with the play. One time, however, during dress rehearsal for the play, I was back stage in the girl's dressing room putting on my costume and stage make-up. Another member of the cast noticed me hanging things up and putting everything back in its place and she said, "Geraldine, I'd hate to see your room, I'll bet it's so neat it's sickening." Then and there it occurred to me that these kids from town had their own private bedrooms. My bed was in the front room of our house. I just didn't say anything. I figured she should have known better.

That summer, I noticed other changes taking place. Boys started hanging around Diana, Lucy, Shirley and me, and actually we didn't mind it too much. The boys slicked down their hair and wore aftershave lotion, whether they needed it or not. And Diana and I went to wearing some of Aunt Mary's expensive perfume she'd left at Grandma Robinette's house after she married "Uncle Carl" and moved to Riverview. The back row of the church, where all of us sat, started smelling like a funeral.

When I went back to the Top of the Hill to listen to the story-telling I was bothered, though, because these changes were taking place too fast. But worst of all, the changes taking place in my life were bypassing Pansy. Sooner or later, I would have to make some hard decisions.

Fortunately, the storytelling hadn't changed, except for the better.

After everybody got their pop and cakes, Daddy got the stories started by telling about a couple up at Wise that owned a store he sold produce to. "Now them two should never a-married, because when they did, it was lightning struck a black gum. Anyway, she was quarreling at him one day for coon hunting so much. Now they liked to quote the Bible to each other to prove their point. So he asked her where in the Good Book did it say that a man wasn't supposed to coon hunt. And she replied that in Jude chapter 2 if she recalled correctly that it said that 'he that layeth and lolygaggeth at night with the hounds is in danger of hell fire and the truth abideth not in him.' Well, the man looked at me and said, 'tell her what it says about women bringing their mothers to live in the same house with her and her husband whom God hath joined together and they have become one flesh.' I told him I didn't recall it saying anything about it. 'Well if it don't, it orta,' he said."

Then Daddy asked if he'd ever told us about the time his Grandpa Cyrus Stallard bought the straight coon dog. Well, Daddy said, he bought this dog and was told that it absolutely wouldn't trash. So he took one of his grandsons with him to try the dog out. The dog barked treed back under a rock, and Grandpa, thinking it was a coon, decided to poke it out with a pole. But the dog had actually run a bobcat under that rock. And the bobcat, instead of running out, grabbed a-hold of Grandpa and bore down. Now his grandson thought he had the coon and ran up and said, "you want me to help you hold him, Grandpa?" "No," Grandpa said, (Grandpa didn't talk real plain) "No," he said, "I jut want you to help me turn him loose."

Grandma Hall said that she remembered them tellin how that Grandpa Stallard had a hard time healing from where the bobcat chewed him up. Then she said people used to use herbs, roots and weeds to doctor with. "People call it folk medicine, and I guess it was because it sure was good medicine for most folk. After the war, Oscar used to get carbuncles, they call them boils now, all over him and they would about pain him to death, nearly. Medical doctors at Walter Reed were unable to do anything for him. They tried but nothing helped. Then Jean's (my mother's) Aunt Liz had me to boil sycamore bark and dock root and give it to him just before bedtime. The next morning his body was covered all over with yellow pimples. But when they dried up, he never had any more boils."

Then Grandma said that Jean's Aunt Tiny had ringworm on her face for over a year. "At least that's what the doctor's said it was. But they couldn't cure it and it turned into a large open sore. Aunt Liz told her to kill a black hen and drip the warm blood on the sore until it was completely covered with blood. She did and the sore healed within days. But the huge scar is there to this day." Grandma added that the warm blood of a black chicken heals erysipelas too. Then Grandma said that you could stop a person from bleeding to death by reading a scripture from Revelations over them.

Daddy said that Beeb Lawson was told to boil beech tree bark and huckleberry bushes for his diabetes, and drink the tea. He used to control his sugar that way. It worked too.

Grandma said that people did whatever they had to. "We used to make all our clothes out of chop sacks. It took two chop sacks to make a dress."

Uncle Victor said that, one time, the Buchanans thought they weren't going to be poor anymore. They were told of a lot of property in England that had belonged to the Buchanans and they were the decendants. A lawyer was hired to check it out.

Aunt Norma told her children that they should thank the Lord above because they had been poor all their live and now they would be rich. But one of her children spoke up and said, "I'm not going to thank Him until I get mine."

Daddy said that back when times were hard, people didn't always have meat to eat so they just ate a lot of soup beans, corn bread, and vegetables. One time when one of his aunts was expecting company for supper, she told the children not to ask for meat because they didn't have any. All they had left was skin. So right in the middle of supper, one of the children held his plate up and said, "Pass the skin, please."

Then Daddy said that Uncle Bob Buchanan, Aunt Lilly's husband, used to tell tall tales to the kids. "One day he told them that there was something in everything you eat to kill you. 'Well why don't you die?' one of them asked. 'Because there's something in everything to cure you,' " he said.

Grandpa Hall said another problem people used to have a long time ago was fires. "They burned bad back then and me and Labourn Lawson were called to fight a big one over in the Flat Woods. We were raking a ring in broom sedge hoping to control it. The fire was getting closer to a woman's house and we was doing everything we could to keep it from burning her house down. After while, she come a-running out and took a pine top and commenced to whomping and beating and put out ten times more fire than me and Labourn both."

I guess fires made Daddy think of cigarettes, so he said that when he was young, boys and girls thought smoking was the thing to do so they rolled their own out of wild plants. "We used rabbit tobacco. We called it Life Everlasting."

Daddy said Labourn Lawson wasn't only a good story teller, he was a real strong man. "One day three of my uncles was trying to lift a log after a log rolling where they had cleared new ground. They couldn't budge the log. After awhile Labourn come along and told them to get out of the way, he would move it for them. He moved the log with ease. One of my uncles said, 'old man, one of these days you're gonna bust your heart right out of you.' Labourn replied, 'Let her rip, bud, they're making them every day and night.' "

Uncle William Buchanan was at the Top of the Hill for that story telling and he said that Oscar (Grandpa Hall) was a strong man too. "When Oscar worked in Holden, West Virginia he was digging in two places and loading two cars in each place. And he still complained about not enough empties (empty cars). One night after loading eight cars, he walked out of the mine and was gonna head home. By Ned, me and Norma lived in Holden then and I begged him to at least come home with me and have some coffee. But Oscar just said, 'The next coffee I have will be Cora's.' And after all of that work, he drove all day to get home."

Then Uncle William said that when he moved to Possum Holler, a man by the name of Ed Reynolds moved into Possum Holler. "Water broke up out of the ground in the edge of a bottom near his house. He decided to case it up to keep out surface water. He found a good sized black gum—a holler tree. He cut off a length of it and burned it inside and out, completely black. Then he dug down to where the water came up out of the ground, sunk the hollow tree and filled back in around it. By Ned, he had the best water that I ever tasted. It was clear and the log lasted more than twenty years."

Then Bob Davis asked if he told anybody about the big ginseng patch he found last year. When everybody said he hadn't, he said that he was crawling through this thicket and gnats was eating him alive. He reached up and pulled a branch off a big bush to knock the gnats off with. When he got through the thicket, he realized he had a branch of a ginseng plant. The thicket turned out to be the biggest ginseng plants that he'd ever heard tell of. He dug the roots and made enough from the sale to build himself a new barn.

June Mead said he found the biggest bunch of ginseng he'd ever found in his life up in the High Knob last year. But the roots run up the hill under a stand of oak trees on the national forest and the first tree he fell getting at the roots, he was arrested by a forest warden that he hadn't seen standing nearby. "I had to pay a hefty fine and didn't even get to bring the seng home and sell it."

Everybody was satisified with that story, so we all commenced to put up our bottles and head home.

The next summer, it became Grandma and Grandpa Hall's turn to take the store at the Top of the Hill. Grandma had never run a store before so Mother and Daddy showed her how to figure percentages to make sure she could mark up her stock and make a profit. But Grandma wasn't overly enthusiastic about that system. One night, after working a long time figuring 10 percent on this and 15 percent on that, Grandma said she didn't worry too much about percents. She told Mother and Daddy that she knew if she bought it for a nickel and sold it for a dime, she'd made money. And that's how Grandma ran the store.

Diana and I got to help in the store. A lot of kids including our little cousins hung around and played marbles, hop scotch, right foot still, hoopy hide, antne over, and jump rope. But we didn't play any games with them because we were too old for that. One day, however, Mother bought a hoola hoop on her way from work. It wasn't long before everybody started acting like kids again. It was funny to watch grown men and women stand with their feet planted about 18 inches apart and their arms outstretched while they moved their middles like merry-go-rounds. I never saw such rotations and gyrations out of humans in all my born days. Before long, almost everyone had hoola hoops.

One day, Carolyn, a little girl from Possum Holler who lived with her grandparents because her daddy was killed in a coal mine and her mother took up with a man who moonshined and made false teeth, came to the store for supplies. Carolyn always brought a list and gave it to the store owners and they delivered the groceries to her grandparents that evening. Mother and Daddy told me that no one ever actually paid for the groceries. Whoever owned the store just put it on account—on account of her grandparents had no money. They said every store had a number of people who had run upon hard times like that, so they "carried" them. Anyway, as Carolyn was about to leave the store, she stopped and watched us twirling the hoola hoop. I asked her would she like to try mine and she shook her head and said, "No, that's okay. Grandma said she's going to get me one for Christmas." Then she turned and walked back down into Possum Holler. Her words went through my heart like a knife through warm butter. I watched her go out of sight down that old dirt road and I realized something right then and there—hollers can be havens or hopples and no one but God knows what makes the difference. Diana and I talked about it all evening, and that night, Grandma and Grandpa delivered a hoola hoop along with other supplies to Carolyn's house. We never really missed it very much. And later on, Carolyn's grandmother said she'd never seen Carolyn have so much fun with anything.

Diana and I had other things on our minds anyway. Grandma Robinette kept pretty cloth at her house and her old treadle sewing machine was always threaded and ready. So one day after Mother left for work, we hopped on bicycles and rode to Grandma Robinette's house. We got some old newspapers and cut patterns and cut material and stitched ourselves some bright, flowered halter tops and shorts. Several times, we'd seen girls strolling around Coeburn in just such get-ups. When we finished, we put those skimpy clothes on and rode back to the store at the Top of the Hill. When Mother came in from work, there I stood in the doorway with my outfit on. Mother looked us over real good and allowed as how we'd done a mighty fine job with the needle and thread. She was sorry, however, that we ran out of material before we ran out of skin. She took us home and made us change. That night she explained to us that she expected we would attract the wrong kind of clientelle to the Top of the Hill if we hung around exposing our wares in that manner. We giggled and let it go. Actually, I had felt a little uncomfortable in the halter top anyway.

DEBBIE
HIGH

Just before summer was over, we walked out the road to eat lunch with Aunt Betty Robinette and our three little cousins because Betty was fixing hamburgers and we hardly ever got that kind of food. Jimmy, our little cousin who was five years old, had learned to read and write, which shouldn't have been a problem, but it was. Every time he saw an advertisement in a magazine or newspaper for anything that said "free" or "free trial offer," he signed his name and address and sent away for it. Aunt Betty and Uncle Maynard were the only people I knew who dreaded seeing the mailman come. So far, they had received a set of melamine dishes, waterless aluminum cookware, all-purpose greeting cards, two Bonnie Lou and Buster albums, an autographed picture of Minnie Pearl, a genuine imitation aligator skin billfold, three life insurance policies, and a hearing aid. I saw Uncle Maynard shake his head once and say, "and just to think that we actually rejoiced when he first learned to write his name." Anyway, we were just finishing our hamburgers when the mailman blew his horn. We all jumped up and ran outside because Diana and I thought these were wonderful diversions. When we got to the road, the smiling mailman handed Aunt Betty a large box then got back into his car and drove away laughing. We didn't have to wonder for long what was inside the box, we could hear it peeping. Jimmy had ordered 50 baby chicks. "Lord have mercy, now he's gone to ordering live things," Aunt Betty said.

While we were helping Aunt Betty fix a place for the baby chicks, one of the younger boys from Possum Holler came running out the road hollering, "Look what I got." He ran up and showed us a squirrel. It was the first one he'd ever killed and he was on his way to the Top of the Hill to show it off. But I looked at Diana and she looked at me because we recognized the small gray squirrel. It was old Otto.

I don't know who started crying first—Diana or me. I sat down in the grass and balled. Aunt Betty realized right away what all the commotion was about, so she explained to the shocked boy that he had just shot a pet squirrel. Then he started crying and the children started crying and Aunt Betty allowed she was in a real mess with 50 live chicks, one dead squirrel, and a whole passel of crying younguns.

The boy dropped the squirrel and his shotgun and ran home, traumatized by the event, and Diana and I finally calmed down enough to try and figure out what we should do. As bad hurt as we were, it was nothing compared to the hurt Pansy would suffer. We both knew that.

We allowed we should take Otto to Pansy's house and give him a magnificent funeral and burial. Otherwise, Pansy would always wonder what happened to him.

Aunt Betty got a shoe box and lined it with red cloth and we placed Otto inside. We wrapped the outside with aluminum foil and stuck a gold christmas bow on it. Then I got a shovel and all of us except Aunt Betty headed for Pansy's house. We picked wildflowers on the way.

Pansy was sitting on the porch when we came in sight and she knew what it was as soon as she saw the box. She'd already missed Otto. We dug a hole beside some hazelnut bushes under Otto's favorite hickory tree, then we placed the shoe box on the porch and began our funeral service. Diana sat beside Pansy and cried and held her hand while I talked about the gates of pearl, streets of gold, and walls of jasper. Then I got a little creative and said they had hickory trees in heaven that bore twelve types of hickory nuts—one for each month of the year. Just before we put the lid on Otto, Pansy took the ribbons from her hair and reached them to me. I placed them in the box. Finally, we sang "All Creatures Great and Small," and our cousins acted as pall bearers and carried that little box across the yard and put it the hole we'd dug and pushed the dirt back over it. Jimmy placed flowers on the grave.

Diana and I had to take the children home but we told Pansy we'd come back later and talk. As we were leaving, Pansy asked her grandma for her notebook. I figured that in a little while some great poetry would flow from Pansy's pain.

That evening I baked corn bread and warmed up soup beans that had been seasoned with streaked meat, and when Mother got home she fried potatoes and killed some onions and lettuce with bacon grease. She sliced tomatoes, got the leftover rhubarb pie out of the refrigerator, and Mother and Daddy and Diana and I sat down to thank God for loving us and for supplying all our needs. Suddenly, I realized that people don't really have a lot of needs. Most of what I had was more than what I needed. So, although I had always thanked God for meeting my needs, I figured I had failed to thank Him for the abundances in my life. From then on, every time I prayed, I tried to thank God for the rhubarb pies in my life, and not just for the soup beans and corn bread. That summer was teaching me a lot.

After supper, we grabbed flashlights and headed for Pansy's house. It wasn't dark then, but we knew it would be dark on the way back. We took three Baby Ruths that Grandma Hall had given us to help us through our mourning. When we got there, Pansy's mother let us in, then she went into the back room where she and Pansy's grandmother went about their quilting. The front room was Pansy's room. Her small iron bed was scooted up against the far wall and beside her bed was a table with "War and Peace," a dictionary, a bible, Emily Dickinson poems, and a bell. At the foot of her bed was a cedar chest with all of her keep sakes. She had let me look in the chest once. Everything Pansy ever put her hands on was in there—even some dried-up flowers that I was afraid to ask about. A chifferobe stood against the wall to the right of the door. And Pansy was sitting in her chair at the short-legged table by the window to the left of the door. We pulled up two big green rockers with multi-colored afghans and sat beside her. A pot-bellied stove stood like an over-stuffed colonel guarding all of us. Soft, evening light fell through the window giving the room a subdued saffron feeling. I don't know when I felt more comfortable.

We started eating the candy and talking. Pansy said she'd watched seven butterflies pass her window during the evening. She was thinking about asking the school teacher if she could borrow a book on butterflies so she could learn to identify them. Then she handed me her notebook. There were three new poems. I read them out loud and when I got to the part about the hair ribbons, we all cried a little. I told Pansy I'd bring old Mutt and Jeff over more often. I hadn't left the coons at Pansy's house too much because you had to fool with the coons a lot, especially after they got old, and Pansy's grandmother didn't care for the bother. And she didn't want Blackjack, the pet crow, around because every time she hung out the wash, he pulled the clothespins off the line and let the washing fall to the ground. She called him ornery.

About that time, we saw Mr. Salyers and his grandson, George, heading around the side of the hill with their old blue tick hound. We figured they were going coon hunting. Diana said she thought George was right good looking. I said I thought his nose was too big. Then Pansy laughed more than I'd seen her laugh in a long time. So I said that if you tried to kiss someone with a nose like a fist, I figured it'd get in the way. Pansy wanted to know how I knew so much about kissing. I hadn't ever kissed a boy and she knew it. If I'd ever done something like that, she'd have known about it because I couldn't keep secrets.

I said "just use your imagination. Would you want some boy's nose smashing into your face while you were trying to kiss?"

But Pansy persisted.

"You must be giving kissing boys a lot of thought."

"I've thought about it, but I'm not sure I'd like it."

Then Diana said maybe we should give it a try. Maybe we should invite George and some other boys to a birthday party and kiss them to see what it was like.

I said I didn't believe it was right to kiss just any boy whose number you happened to draw, or who a spinning bottle pointed toward. And anyway, neither of us was sixteen years old yet. you had that kind of party when you turned sixteen.

Diana hadn't known about the "sixteen" rule. And she said I was probably right about a girl not kissing a boy before she liked him.

"How long would it take you to like George," Pansy asked.

"You sure are full of questions," Diana said.

We laughed so hard, I nearly choked on my Baby Ruth.

Diana said she had heard about this boy and girl in Norfolk who both wore braces on their teeth. When they kissed, their braces hung together and their parents had to take them to the hospital to get them separated.

"How humiliating," Pansy yelled.

That remark brought her grandmother running into the room asking what was the matter.

We couldn't think of anything to say except, "nothing." Then we sat there and stared at the ceiling trying to look as innocent as possible. Her grandmother left the room shaking her head. Then Pansy patted her temple with her finger and said, "It seemed like the right thing to do." And we laughed some more.

Before long, Pansy's Mother said it was time for her to go to bed, so we got our flashlights and left.

On the way home, Diana told me that Rodney Lawson liked me, she could tell by the way he hung around me at church. I said I guess I hadn't been paying attention. We laughed some more. Then I asked Diana why she didn't tell me about Rodney at Pansy's house.

"You know why," was all she said.

CHAPTER 13

SAVED, SEALED, SANCTIFIED, AND SOAKED

Just before Diana went back to Norfolk, we had the big baptising in Clear Creek up at Ramsey. We had to get everyone baptised that was saved in our good revival meeting. Most of the time, Presbyterians sprinkled rather than immerse. But the people at the Top of the Hill came from Freewill backgrounds and they wanted to be "put under." Up the creek from where we were baptising were some "Jesus Only" people. They were baptising converts too. They baptised in the name of Jesus only because they read in Acts where the apostles baptised some people that way. Before our baptising commenced, the candidates (for baptism) gathered on the creek bank with preacher Ruff. The women wore raincoats over their dresses and the men wore their Sunday go-to-meeting suits. Mother, Daddy, Claude Hays, and Beeb Lawson gathered down by the creek and began to sing in four part harmony, "Home on the Banks of the River."

> *There's a beautiful home*
> *beyond the dark river*
> *there's a mansion by faith I can see*
> *and the Savior is there*
> *His faithful to welcome*
> *there's a beautiful home for me.*

> *Chorus*

> *Home, sweet home, on the banks of the river*
> *home, yes home, where the ransomed ones gather*
> *home, for me, with the angels forever*
> *on the beautiful banks of the river*

Then one by one, preacher Ruff began taking the converts into the water, about waist high, reading scripture and baptising them in the name of the Father, Son, and Holy Ghost. Between each baptising, the quartet continued singing as the convert came shouting up out of the water. Each time, preacher Ruff, in his powerful baritone voice yelled, "Glory be." Families met their saved, sealed, sanctified, and soaked loved ones at the water's edge with tears and towels.

It occurred to me that earth holds no harmony like the union of nature with humankind, finite with infinite, the everlasting with the temporal, the creator with the created. And when these earthly voices blended and united with the sweet-flowing waters of creation on that river bank, it produced an angelic concert that could not be contained nor written, only experienced. It reminded me of last Sunday's sermon, how that before the fall, Adam and Eve had only fellowship with God, but now, we could be united with God through Jesus Christ.

And sometime during the baptising, that union occurred. A jubilation rose in the souls of everyone on the river bank and for a moment in time, God drew back the dark curtain of separation and allowed us to experience His glory. As the crescendo continued, everyone who hadn't been saved in the meeting was saved on the spot and baptised. The Jesus Only group wound up at our baptising and people that lived nearby walked over, and everyone said they had never seen nor heard anything like it.

On the way home, Diana asked me if I noticed that Rodney Lawson got baptised. I said I had noticed.

And she said, "Well?"

I said it seemed to make his daddy real happy.

Then she grinned and said, "You know what I mean."

I just smiled, because I didn't hardly know what to make of these new events.

Several weeks later, Hortense Hale, Allen Hale's wife, brought pictures of the baptising to church with her. There was a halo around the head of pastor Ruff. It was as clear as day.

That winter, the church Christmas plays were better than ever. The Freewill Baptist church on the lower end of Dry Fork produced "The Prodigal Son." In the swine scene, squeeling and grunting hogs' heads appeared above wooden boards fashioned to look like a real sty. As those two big boars chomped and oinked, their mouths opened and closed around slobbery tongues and half-chewed corn. Big floppy ears moved just enough to look real. Two of the Brooks brothers wore the hand-made costumes and played the pigs. And when it was over, everybody said they were real hams. Of course, the most touching scene was when the prodigal son "came to himself" and arose and returned home to his father who ran to meet him and embraced him. After the play, the congregation sang together:

> I will arise and go to Jesus
> He will embrace me in his arms
> In the arms of my dear savior
> Oh there are ten thousand charms

The plays at the church on Dry fork had been started years earlier by Aunt Lizy and Uncle Ballard Robinette. Although they loved children, they were never blessed with any of their own. So they did a lot of work in the church with the young people. Aunt Lizy wrote and directed all of their Christmas plays until she passed away. The church continued the tradition of those plays because everyone in several communities had come to expect it from them.

At the Top of the Hill, we decided to do a play about a Christmas angel who helped a wealthy family find the real meaning of Christmas. We usually ordered our plays from a man in Tennessee who wrote Christmas plays and advertised them in Southern Planter magazine. Anyway, Mother had asked me to go to the churchhouse early each day and build the fire so we could be warm during rehearsals. One evening, I changed out of my school clothes and walked up to the church and while I was building the fire, I heard somebody walk through the door. I glanced around and saw it was Rodney Lawson. I said, "You're here a little early, aren't you?" Then I turned and closed the stove door. When I turned back around, Rodney was standing as close to me as whiskers on a cat's face. We stared, almost cross-eyed, at each other for a second, then our lips just met. It didn't seem like either of us moved toward the other, but I guess he must have moved. For about two seconds, which was just enough time for my blood to turn to dish-water, our lips touched. I don't know why I didn't pull away and slap him or something. Of course, the hot stove was behind me so I couldn't have moved very far. When he pulled back and we looked at each other, I was so bumfuzzled, I stammered, "So, you got baptised last summer."

He stuck his hands in his coat pockets and said, "Yeah, a lot of us did."

"I was there."

"I know, I saw you," he said.

I sat down on the front pew trying to think of something else to say because silence didn't seem appropriate. He propped one foot on the lip of the stove and looked up at the ceiling. Somehow, in the silence, I became aware of an accumulation of liquid in my mouth and I got a strong urge to swallow. But it was so quiet in there, I thought a swallow would probably sound like old faithful erupting. I was afraid to say anything because, by then, so much spit had accumulated in my mouth that I knew I would gargle my words, or worse yet, slobber. I wondered if anyone had ever strangled to death in this situation. We both remained in the same positions for several minutes until I heard Mother and some other church ladies coming through the door. I jumped up and ran to meet them. They were carrying costumes and props for the play. I noticed that Rodney stuck his hands over the stove as though he'd just come in out of the cold and was trying to warm them. Mother glanced at me and glanced at him but never said anything. Of course, every evening from then on, Mother was through with her work in plenty of time to accompany me to the churchhouse and build the fire.

Because of play practice, I didn't get to go to Pansy's house until Saturday. But Saturday morning, Mother dropped me off while she took Pansy's mother and grandmother to trade. Pansy was sitting in her chair by the window. I picked up "War and Peace" and sat down in the rocking chair and casually flipped through the pages. I didn't want to say anything to Pansy right away, but I couldn't help it. I closed the book and just blurted out, "Rodney Lawson kissed me in church Tuesday evening."

Pansy's eyes got bigger than half dollars, "You don't mean it," she said. "Well, what was it like?"

"His lips were cool and a little wet. We barely touched and it just lasted a second or two."

"What did you do?'

"Nothing. Do you think I should have slapped him?"

"For kissing you in a churchhouse? Goodness no."

"What's being in a churchhouse got to do with it?"

"Well, It must have been ordained of God or something."

"Pansy, I don't think God had anything to do with it."

We both laughed.

"Did you close your eyes?"

"Either I closed my eyes or God struck me blind, because I didn't see anything while it happened."

"Are you going to do it again?"

"I doubt it. I think Mother will stick to me like Elisha to Elijah until I turn sixteen."

"Now you won't be able to say 'sweet sixteen and never been kissed'."

"That was not one of my top priorities in life."

"But it's a noble goal."

Pansy giggled.

Then I said, "Really, what do you think about it?"

Pansy pecked her temple a long time and said, "It seemed like the right thing to do."

After we both laughed and I gave the rocker a push and heaved a deep sigh to prove my sincerity and thoughtfulness on the subject, I said, "Pansy, how do you fall in love? Is it being in the right place at the right time? Does it strike you like a bolt of lightning out of nowhere and you're stuck with the first person who happens into view? Or is it something mysterious and slow, like a river?"

Pansy said she believed love was mysterious but it wasn't necesarrily slow. "It may sweep over someone like a raging river and carry them along on a current of fury until it tosses them against the jagged rocks of the rapids or buries them in the deep swirling waters," she said, her voice rising dramatically to the jagged rocks and then falling into the swirling waters. "Or, it may deposit its passenger safely on some peaceful shore, far away from the dangers of the roaring tide." Then Pansy indicated that she didn't think the latter happened too often.

I told Pansy that I didn't know love was that dangerous and I didn't know she knew so much about it. Pansy gave me a very satisfied look and said, "I know just about everything." And I believe she did. She had gathered experience and knowledge of the ages from her books. And God had given Pansy special insight, I believe, into unseeable worlds, and He had given her something else—time to contemplate and understand. I was chasing through life like snow in March. And, for the first time ever, I envied her.

The Christmas play was a hit. Everybody liked the plot because it took an angel and a poor family to open the eyes of the wealthy. When Santa Claus handed out Christmas presents, my name was called a second time. I got a box of candy and all it said was, "from a secret admirer." Lucy and Shirley also got extra presents. Theirs didn't have names either. I figured the extra present at Christmas routine was the first rite of passage for us. And although it was exciting, I still wasn't sure I was looking for any kind of passage. I just didn't like change.

After the play and gift giving, we took Pansy home. She opened her presents there. She got a box of chocolate covered cherries, jackrocks, dominoes, a set of fine point writing pens, hair ribbons, a doll with a bottle and a little quilt, and my present. I got her a field guide to butterflies. The doll was from Pansy's grandmother and she had made the little quilt by hand. After Pansy opened all her presents, her grandmother went into the back room and brought out a big quilt and gave it to her. It matched the little doll's quilt. I got an uneasy feeling that I couldn't understand, but I bragged on it like everyone else.

Then Pansy's mother said she better go to bed, so we got ready to leave. When I reached the door, I looked back at Pansy and a strained glance passed between us. Somehow, the night seemed a lot colder as we left Pansy's house than it did when we got there.

It didn't take people very long to figure out who got me the box of candy. Rodney started sitting beside me in church every Sunday. He found out I liked teaberry chewing gum so he always kept me well supplied. Everybody seemed to think it was only natural that Rodney and I kept company. After all, his daddy had sung in the Mt. Olivet quartet with Claude Hays and my mother and daddy since we were children. Still, we hadn't hung around together as children, so it wasn't all that natural for me. Rodney started sleigh riding with our group at the top of the hill. He had always rode with a group in Crab Orchard that all piled onto a 1950 Ford car hood and rode down the side of a mountain. Everybody who rode down mountains always said the '50 Ford hoods made the best toboggins of anything they'd ever tried. People who had '50 fords had to be careful, for quite often, they had missing hoods.

I wasn't hardly sixteen years old and Mother wouldn't let me date till I reached that magic birthday. And, anyway, Rodney didn't have a vehicle. So he rode his bike to my house every Friday night and visited. Somehow, it seemed awkward when he just walked in and sat around, so we started playing guitars and singing together. Mother and Daddy usually sat around with us until about 10 p.m. then they went on to bed and Rodney stayed until 11 p.m.

One Saturday evening, Daddy got home from selling produce and it occurred to me that he was having to get up at four on Saturday mornings to begin his route in Kentucky. So, while we were eating supper, I told Daddy that I had forgotten how early he'd been getting up on Saturdays. Then I asked if mine and Rodney's singing on Friday nights was bothering him. Before he could answer, Mother spoke up and said, "No, your singing doesn't bother us at all, but those long quiet spells sure do." I didn't say anything else through the rest of supper.

Actually, our long quiet spells were usually discussions about the future. Rodney was in his first year at Clinch Valley College and hoped to transfer to the University of Virginia after his second year. And he didn't plan on coming back to the mountains to live and work. He was good in math and wanted to be an engineer. I'd be graduating from high school next year, but I wasn't looking forward to it, because, although I liked the idea of getting an education, I didn't want to leave the mountains. So my path and his path didn't seem compatible.

Rodney knew about Pansy being my special friend, and he said she was why I didn't want to leave. I told him that Pansy was part of the reason, but I had been planted in the mountains and that was where I wanted to sprout and blossom. Sometimes we almost argued over the merits of staying and leaving. But Rodney was smart, and I told him that with or without me, he should go on and get an education and try to "get as far above his raising as he could." We laughed over that because he had been told that was what he was doing. The only problem Rodney had was that the mining business had turned bad right after Rodney's daddy opened a mine of his own. Rodney had saved a little money hoeing gardens for people, and he got a Slemp Foundation scholarship. But there wasn't any way his family could help him financially.

CHAPTER 14

SOME LEAVIN AND SOME STAYIN

After Rodney and I started hanging around together, I became part of the group of young people that would be leaving. It seemed strange that people would divide into groups of those who would stay and those who would leave, but that's what happened. I didn't feel comfortable in my leaving group, but I didn't feel part of the staying group either.

It seemed like I was in a one-way tunnel, sandwiched between the ones in front and the ones behind. Stone-faced people on the sidelines kept motioning us forward, faster and faster. I checked the faces in my pool, and they appeared to be urging me forward too. But I figured that somewhere up ahead, this tunnel would have an exit, and I'd be able to break free and go my own path if I chose to. Of course, I knew that the longer I stayed on this road, the farther back it'd be. By now, my own mother and daddy and all my grandparents were expecting me to go to college and leave the mountains.

Diana came in that summer on a Thursday. So I called Rodney and he said he could bring his cousin, Ron, with him for our Friday night date. Diana and I baked cookies before they came to the house. Then we got dressed up in white blouses and full skirts and bobby socks and splashed "To a Wild Rose" in every dimple on our bodies. Rodney and Ron came in drenched in Old Spice. As we moved around, the rose mixed with the spice and made the room smell like autumn leaves burning. We played records and danced. We didn't step it off. We danced the jitterbug, the twist, and the stroll to Little Richard, Chubby Checker, and Fats Domino. Mother and Daddy thought they'd never seen such a funny sight. Mother didn't mind those dances. She figure that after we finished several hours of that, we'd be too tired to get into any kind of trouble. Diana told Ron that she knew Rodney and I liked each other before we knew it ourselves. She and Ron never did hit it off but they were both good dancers, so they spent the summer together, with Rodney and me. And Shirley and Lucy and their boyfriends sometimes joined us and we'd spend the evening dancing and making and eating candy.

One slithery summer morning, however, a pronouncement shattered the walls of my world. The telephone rang and it was Grandma Robinette calling from the hospital. She had called the ambulance for Grandpa, but he never made it to the hospital. He went peaceful, she said, the way he prayed he would. He always prayed that God would take him before he smothered to death, and God honored his request.

He was the first of my grandparents to die. The doctor said his heart had worked too hard, too long. That was because Grandpa had black lung disease from the coal mine complicated by bouts of asthma.

Diana and I figured Grandpa's lungs might have been black but his heart was pure white. For Grandpa never uttered an ill word about anybody. You couldn't mention a soul but what Grandpa told you something good about them. At the wake, the night before the funeral, everybody talked about how we could have stood more of his kind in the world. He was a gentle man and a gentleman, everybody said.

Grandpa's funeral was held in the chapel of the funeral home in Coeburn. It had become right popular to hold funerals there. I guess it was easier that way. It was at Grandpa's funeral that I noticed the difference in crying. When somebody gets hurt physically, they cry in pain—it's more like squalling or shrieking. but when someone mourns, when the pain rises out of a broken heart, all they can do is whimper or groan. Sometimes it builds to a wail. But that kind of pain can't be expressed with an ordinary cry.

It also occured to me that death is not natural. We were created to live forever. Every cell, every atom of our bodies yearns for eternal life. Death is the result of sin entering into the world and snatching away our Eden. I understood right then that all the good words and explanations in the world will never help us accept the overtaking shadow of death.

Grandpa was buried at Temple Hill cemetery at Castlewood rather than in the Robinette graveyard. Most family graveyards were about full and they were getting harder to keep up. People just didn't have the time to work on them, like they once did. At Temple Hill the deceased got perpetual care. Families didn't have to worry about it at all. Of course, we knew Grandpa's soul was getting perpetual care around the throne of God.

At church that Sunday we sang "Precious Memories":

Precious mem'ries, unseen angels
Sent from somewhere to my soul
How they linger, ever near me
And the sacred past unfold

Precious father, loving mother
Fly across the lonely years
And old home scenes of my childhood
In fond memory appears

Chorus
Precious mem'ries, how they linger
How they ever flood my soul

110

In the stillness of the midnight
Precious, sacred scenes unfold.

Diana and I talked about the good times we'd had with Grandpa that we would never have again—not on this side of eternity anyway. How sweet it would have been to have Grandpa play "Going Up Cripple Creek," one more time. And we didn't even learn how he made animal shadows on the wall with his hands. I spent several nights writing down some of the stories Grandpa told, because I was afraid I'd forget them. Always before, when something bothered me, Mother reminded me that the Bible says, "and it came to pass." It never says "and it came to stay." But she didn't say it this time and I think that's because the hurt from losing a grandpa never passes.

When you're young, days are like ballet in slow motion, but by the time you're almost grown, they speed by like signposts along the highway. Before you can read them, they're gone. And so were the days of summer, that year. Time grew restless and snapped her fingers to a quickened tempo and we, we grew the necessary wings. We swam, we danced, we picnicked; we laughed and cried, we sang and prayed—all in one beat. Ocassionally, the tempo tarried at church, the Top of the Hill, or Pansy's house. One evening, we went to the Top of the Hill to watch our horseshoe pitching champions defend their title against the Dry Fork champions, and after the match, we had one of the best story-tellings since Noah gathered his grandchildren around him and told them about the flood.

Diana and I got a bottle of pop each and potato chips and sat back to listen. Daddy got the stories started off by saying that Will Robinette, my grandpa, bought the first car (a model T Ford) on Dry Fork. He was coming back from Coeburn one day when it quit on him. It only had a built-in crank to turn the motor, no electric starter. "After Will was completely worn out trying to crank the car, he decided to demolish it. He found a large rock and was going to toss it through the windshield. The rock was heavy and he only got it on the hood. The rock glanced off without much damage so he decided to try and crank it one more time. One turn was all it took of the crank and it fired right up."

Daddy said that John Robinette bought the car from Will but he didn't know much about driving so Will was teaching him one night after they got in from the mine. "John had on a mining cap and carbide lamp and the car had magnita lights. John drove slow but still couldn't see the road. He finally ran out of the road and into the fence. Will told him to put the light out, but he said he had to have that carbide light burning so he could see the 'chinery.' "

"Back then," Daddy said, "almost all cars were Fords (T models) with a cloth top stretched from the top of a very high windshield to a straight back. One day, a neighbor of ours bought a hard-top car. They called it a glass top car. It had roll up windows instead of the curtains the first cars had. It was so shiny you could see yourself in it. But when he parked the car between the house and barn, his old milk cow got to looking at it and when she come closer, she saw her reflection and thought it was another cow. She took a run and go and rammed it and nearly tore the side out, and it brand new. Light top cars were later called touring cars."

Uncle Maynard said that, years ago, Arthur Davis bought a car called a Whippet. One night after church meeting when it wouldn't crank, Albert Hall told him to whip it and maybe it would go. He said "I believe it's been whipped too much now."

Elbert Day's car stalled on him in a curve at his Dad's (Grandpa Robinette's) house, Uncle Maynard said. "The curve was stiff and the hollow, down below the road, was deep. Elbert asked Dad to come and give him a push over the hill, meaning down the road. When Dad gave him a shove, the wheels were turned wrong and the car actually went into the deep hollow. Elbert later said that he'd never again ask Will Robinette to push him over the hill."

June Meade said that cars used to be hard to crank after severely cold nights. "Well, Velma Hensley put an imitation fur coat on her car hood one cold night hoping to keep it from freezing up. The hood was damp and the next morning when she went to pull the coat off, it wouldn't hardly come but when it did, the fur stuck to the hood. rather than getting mad about her ruined coat, Velma looked it over and told the family that the car had 'haired over' during the night."

Daddy said they used to make a car called the Jewett. "It was one of the biggest cars made back then. And Jean's Aunt Prudy who was married to Uncle Ed Wilson, had a son and daughter called Roy and Dell. They lived on Dry Fork and you know the road is narrow down through there—hardly any wide places at all. But Dell bought herself a Jewett car. There were no turning places for big cars on Dry Fork, so when she headed for Coeburn, she had to go whichever direction the Jewett was headed. If it was headed down Dry Fork, she went around by Bull Run and into Coeburn. If the car was headed up Dry Fork, she went through Crab Orchard and into Coeburn. Of course, in Coeburn she could get home going either direction—so the car was headed first one way and the other.

Grandpa Hall said that people used to hitch rides any time a car came through, and instead of actually getting into the car, they'd just step onto the running board and hang on. "One time

Noah Medley of Medley's Funeral Home in Coeburn sent his hearse to Dry Fork to pick up a woman in labor. On the way, the driver picked up Little Doc Dingus who just hung onto the running board. You all know Doc Dingus looked pale and frail anyhow; so as they were passing through Crab Orchard, one of the Bond men saw them coming and ran to the road waving and hollering, 'Hey, you're losing your corpse, you're losing your corpse.' The hearse driver stopped and told him, he didn't have no corpse at all—that was Doc Dingus and he was going out on a labor case. 'Now, what do you know about that,' the Bond man told his family, 'some fool has done gone and worked hisself to death."

Uncle Victor said that two men were traveling through West Virginia one time before they put bridges over streams. "So they come upon a sign that said 'open Ford ahead.' Well they decided that meant to floor the old T-model. And when they come to the creek, they took to the air and plopped down right in the middle of it and killed the engine."

Uncle Maynard said he was riding with a boy one time, helping him take off a load of coal. All of a sudden at an intersection, the boy stuck his head out the window and yelled "ya hoo" to the top of his lungs and then floored the old coal truck. Uncle Maynard asked him what in the world he was doing. The boy said he was just obeying the highway sign, and it clearly said "Yell for right of way." Uncle Maynard said they had just passed a new "yield right of way" sign.

Then Daddy said that when synthetic rubber car tires first come out it was called "thinthetic" by a lot of people, because they didn't like it.

Grandpa Hall spoke up and said, "You all know how steep the hills are in West Virginia. Well, some men traveling through West Virginia on a narrow winding road, rounded a curve, and saw something big fall into the road ahead of them. They stopped and to their surprise, it was a man. So they got out and asked the man what was going on. He said, 'Lordy mercy, this makes twice already this morning that I've fallen out of my cornfield.' "

Then Grandpa said that when he was growing up, their fields were so steep that they couldn't use wagons to haul the corn to the barn, they had to use sleds. And the sleds would have run into the mules, except they wrapped log chains around the front of the runners to keep them from hitting the mules. They called it "rough locks."

"The other day," Grandpa said, "I passed a man plowing his corn. The weeds and the sprouts were so thick he could hardly see where the row was. So he said to the old mule, 'Gee a little, I think.' "

It was time for everyone to stand up and stretch and get

more pop or cake and after milling around a little and talking about one of the Dry Fork boys getting mean enough to fight a buzz saw, we sat back down and listened for more.

Daddy said that back during the late 1930's, he was hitchhiking around everywhere looking for work. He got into Akron, Ohio one night and asked the first man he saw where he could find a clean room, cheap. The man told him to go over to the hotel across the street. They had rooms for twenty-five, thirty, and thirty-five cents. "I didn't want to splurge, so I said, 'I'll take a thirty-cent room.' It was more of a stall than a room. It had a small metal bed against one wall and just enough space to walk between it and the other wall. It had a shelf over the bed where you could put your clothes. But it seemed clean and had a good clean shower down the hall. But I still don't know what the twenty-five cent room must have been like."

Uncle Victor said that during the 30's, two men stopped in a honky tonk in War, West Virginia one Saturday night. When they went inside, the juke box was playing "Maple on the Hill." When that song ended, they decided to play something else. They walked over to the machine and put a nickel in and started to punch a button. Someone tapped them on the shoulder and said, "Maple on the Hill." They said they had already heard that song and wanted something else. But after more men walked up and pointed to "Maple on the Hill," they punched that button and sat down. They stayed an hour or longer and when they left, "Maple on the Hill" was still playing.

Daddy said that back around 1950, airplane flying got right popular in Coeburn. And anybody could fly that wanted to. So Edgar Davis flew a lot and Junior Holbrook loved to fly. Junior got right good at flying and one day he rented a plane and flew under an electric wire and flew so low that he landed with a willow branch hung on one of the landing gears.

June Meade said he remembered when they had an air show out at Coeburn and Edgar was the announcer for it. Edgar told the crowd that Sergeant Bantam was going to parachute out of a plane. So everybody gathered in close to see it, and the plane circled and circled and finally something came tumbling to earth. The parachute opened and to everyone's amazement there was a bantam rooster on the end of it.

They kept telling stories from the 30's, 40's and 50's until Daddy finally said that it was a mountain boy that played an important role in World War II. "Fred and Kate Hall from Dry Fork had a son, Maynard Hall. Maynard went off to college and got as much education as he could in science. Then he got a job at Oak Ridge Tennessee. When he come home to visit, he couldn't talk about what it was he was developing. But later, people learned that he was instrumental in the development of the atomic bomb."

Everybody agreed that mountain people were sharp as they could be, but didn't use to have much of a chance to get an education and become somebody.

By that time, people were stretching and yawning and saying they better get on down to Possum Holler. It had been a good night.

Finally one idle evening, just before Diana went back to Norfolk, we walked up to the Top of the Hill to get a bottle of pop and sit around a while. The pop wasn't as good as it used to be because it wasn't kept crystally cold in an old red ice cooler. It was kept in an electric cooler. We both got Dr. Peppers because Grandma had found wads of chewed tobacco, bees, spiders, rags, and ugly gobs of slimy stuff in about every other drink. She kept the unopened contaminated bottles sitting on the window sill above the pop cooler. And every time somebody got a bottle of pop out of the cooler and started to open it, Grandma shook her head at them, then she took the bottle from their hand and held it up to the window. Like a chemist with a Ph.D., she turned the bottle round and round, shaking it a little from time to time, while she scrutinized it for foreign matter. If she decided it was safe, she handed it back to the person and nodded for them to continue. But she always pointed to the polluted bottles on the window sill and said, "I've never found a filthy Dr. Pepper bottle yet." Finally, most everyone started drinking Dr. Peppers. The other bottling companies offered to buy the dirty drinks from her, but she refused to sell.

We took our Dr. Peppers and sat down on the steps in front of the door to watch our little cousins play. They'd been playing hoopie hide and right foot still, but when we went outside they began playing games with songs and chants. They garnished the hot evening air with their tiskets and taskets and handkerchiefs full of buttermilk, London bridge was rebuilt, the farmer took a wife, and hi-o-the-deary-o, the bone stood alone. A steady stream of miners began stopping by the store to pick up their linament, canned biscuits, and laying mash. We moved off and back onto the steps to let them in and out of the door. Finally, the children began chanting "Ring around the Rosy." Pansy had read a book, not long before, about Mother Goose Rhymes, and told me that "Ring around the Rosy" was about the black plague, probably the bubonic plague, that killed so many people in Europe in the fourteenth century. I was thinking about that just as Buddy McCoy's daddy rounded the sand-cut bend below the store on the Crab Orchard side and headed up the road. I had never noticed before, just how stooped over he was. He stopped in the store, bought a 50 pound bag of feed, heaved it onto that begrudging shoulder, and headed on down Possum Holler. I watched his slow, deliberate steps plod out of sight—he was bent clear to the waist, and he never did straighten up. All the while, the children kept chanting, "ashes to ashes, we all fall down—ashes to ashes . . ."

A sick feeling started from the pit of my stomach and radiated up through my face and head like a swarm of bees. My hair even felt sick. I had to go inside and lie down a few minutes. Later that evening, I asked Daddy if he'd noticed how Amos McCoy had gotten all stooped over lately. Daddy said, "Oh, you must have seen him coming from the coal mine. He works every day in 28 inches of coal. After he gets out of the mine, he usually can't straighten his back until he's almost home." Daddy said Allen Hale, Wallace Bond, and a lot of the miners were working in coal so low that they had to crawl on their hands and knees into the mine while carrying their lunch buckets in their teeth. But Amos McCoy, being older, had a back that had taken about all the hard work it could handle. I felt my stomach roll over again. That night, I told Diana that I reckoned the black plague of the mountains must be coal.

In church that Sunday we sang, "Farther on."[1]

> Farther on, still go farther
> Count the milestones one by one
> Jesus will never forsake you never
> It gets better, farther on.

I wondered how many milestones Buddy McCoy's daddy would have to pass before it got better. The very last one, I suspected.

Somewhere, down deep in my soul, I knew the Appalachian mountains had offered up all it possibly could for me, and for all of us. It had brought us forth, and for us it was emptied and poured out. But the process was killing both the mountains and its people. I knew at last it was time to bid it farewell and pray to God that somehow we could be healed and restored before "we all fell down."

1. Reprinted by permission of the publisher, R.E. Winsett Music Co.

CHAPTER 15

THE FINAL GATHERING

The next summer was both disappointing and exciting. Everyone was still talking about Francis Gary Powers, one of the mountain boys, getting shot down over Russia in his U-2 spy plane. They liked the idea of one of our own being involved in international espionage, but they thought the government was bungling the whole episode. There was talk that we would have to send a mountain lawyer to bring him back home.

And we couldn't go swimming at the Rock Hole anymore. Several children, who had gone swimming in Guest's River the past summer, wound up with ear infections and the doctor said it was because the water was polluted. Signs were posted and people were told to stop swimming in it because they could get infectious diseases. One day, Rodney and I walked down to the river. Along the railroad tracks, the smell of hot tar and creosote and the mighty roaring sound broadcast from the rocky bluff behind the river were as alluring as ever. Climbing down the cliffs, I saw something shiny in the dirt beneath a honeysuckle bush. As I looked closer, I realized it was an old gold hairbow of mine. I must have lost it when I was six or seven years old. I started to dig it out of the dirt, then I decided to leave it alone. Sometime in the distant future, when the rivers would all flow clean again, when creation could hug herself and God could smile, I wanted some little girl to find that hairbow and know she had returned to an old path, where joys are built upon joys and sorrows upon sorrows in the eternal cycle of things. We climbed on down the cliff to the river. Beer cans cluttered the ground where we used to spread our picnics. The river looked and acted the same, as though it was unaware of its ill-gained reputation. As we stood on the little rock at the upper end of the hole and gazed at its placid blue fury, I told Rodney that a river is a tribute to life, a fanfare, an applause; a mother that protests and scolds and invites us to pause and reflect. If we violate her purity, her virtue, we will regret it for ever and ever. Rodney looked sincere and nodded, but I believe he was thinking that a sewage treatment plant and a little work on mine run-off would fix the pollution—no big deal. We walked home without saying much, just holding hands—our minds miles apart.

I was excited about going into the twelfth grade at Coeburn high school and about Rodney finishing his second year at Clinch Valley. Louder than ever, I kept telling everyone that I would never leave the mountains, not for good, at least. But Rodney and I had just about decided to get married after I graduated. Then I could work while he finished his engineering degree at the University of Virginia. It seemed like the right thing to do. But to anyone who asked, I repeated that I would never leave.

On the fourth of July, Mother, Daddy, Rodney, and I took a picnic over to Pansy's house and ate and sang songs and talked and laughed. Pansy teased Rodney about his crew cut and he teased Pansy and me about our love of chocolate cake. Finally, Mother and Daddy and Rodney left, but I stayed to write some poetry with Pansy. We thought we might write about chocolate.

While we were writing, Pansy wanted to know what it felt like to be a senior in school. I told her I didn't know yet, but I thought it wouldn't feel much different. It must feel different, she said, because it marks the end of many years of matriculation. We laughed because Pansy loved to toss around latinate words when she talked about education. We wrote a little more and then she looked at me and said, "And it marks the beginning of a new life."

No it doesn't, I said. I like my life just the way it is—no endings, no new beginnings. There may be some interruptions, but no permanent changes. We continued to write our chocolate poetry, saying things like, "I fudged a little on this one." Then Pansy said, "Geraldine, there's a place in the Atlantic Ocean called the Sargasso Sea—a calm place. But it's bad for ships because there's not enough wind for their big sails and they get all tangled up in gulf weed. They can't escape once they're trapped that way . . . so, they stay there till they die." I looked at her, but she was looking down, writing. I looked over on the table to see if she had been reading a book about pirates because, of course, something about a place with no wind would catch her attention. But still, it seemed strange that she'd come up with something like that right out of the blue. She never looked up so I went back to my writing. Finally, we read our limericks, lyrics, and jingles about chocolate and talked about how you just couldn't seem to get serious about a bean that grows on a cacao tree. Then I hugged her and left because Rodney and I were visiting my grandma Robinette that night. Diana didn't come in for the summer because she had a boyfriend. So Grandma liked for Rodney and me to visit and talked about all the funny things we used to do together. I liked to talk about it too. It brought back good times.

One evening just before school started back, Mother and Daddy and I were eating dinner when Daddy said that Grandma and Grandpa Hall were tired of running the store and they'd be leaving it in a few weeks and moving back down into Possum Holler. "Who's going to run it?" I asked.

"Nobody," Daddy said.

I looked up from my plate and said, "Nobody? Why, somebody has to run it. They can't just close it down."

"There's no profit in it," Daddy said. "As a matter of fact, it's been losing money for a long time."

"But what will people do, I mean, the ones who don't have any money, the ones who put their groceries on account. What will they do for food now?"

"Government programs, commodities, food stamps. They won't do without."

"What about everyone else?"

"You see," Daddy said, "Most everybody is doing their trading in town at the supermarket. About all they're buying at the Top of the Hill is an item or two when they run out of something during the week. And for people who aren't particular how they make their money, there's plenty to be made in the food stamp business." Then Daddy said that some people were saying that they could get the stamps, take them to certain stores where they could trade them for cash—not as much cash as they were worth in groceries. Then the store owner turned them in for full value. Everybody made money that way. "People say corruption is riding into the mountains on the back of government aid," he said.

"But what about . . ." I just let it go. Time, like the tide, erodes the land. I figured that's why we shouldn't build too near the shore. And I'd never do it again.

Just after school started back, I went to the Top of the Hill for the last story telling I would ever be privileged to attend. Everybody was there, but you couldn't tell it was the last gathering. They were laughing and as happy as ever.

June Mead got the stories started by saying that he once had an uncle who was a Singer sewing machine salesman. "Yeah, my uncle, he got a job with Singer, a-selling door to door. Well, he went to this one house way back in the mountains and a woman came to the door and he showed her his sewing machine and asked her wouldn't she like to have one to help her with all her handiwork. She said she would love to have it, but he'd have to see her husband who was working up in the field behind the house. He took his demonstrator machine and tredged up the side of the hill and saw a man working in the field like she said, but when he got closer, he saw that he was a colored man. He looked all over the hillside and never saw anybody else so he went back to the house and told the woman he couldn't find her husband, all he saw was a colored man a-working up there in the field. 'That's my husband,' she said.

'You mean, you being a white woman, you're married to a colored man?' he said.

'That's nothing, but I got a sister who really done bad.'

'You have. Who in the world did she marry?'

'A Singer sewing machine salesman,' she said as she left him standing on the porch a-holding his demonstrator in his hand."

Daddy said they used to pedal sewing machines, churns, and

even eye glasses door to door, and that was pretty good work, so an eye-glass salesman came through once going house to house with samples of frames. "When he stopped at William Bond's house, Aunt Sally said that she needed a pair of glasses. So Uncle William handed her a pair of frames and told her 'Solly,' he called her Solly—'Solly, try these on and see if they help your vision.' She put them on and looked out the window at the hillside, then looked at some reading and replied, 'Why William, I can see a lot better with these than I can with my natural eye.' "

Sometimes their storytelling turned into whoppers where each tried to outdo the other but this time they just kept telling whatever popped into their minds, it seemed. Labourn was ponderously quiet, so it was Daddy, Uncle Victor, Uncle Maynard, and June Mead who seemed to be in a big way to tell stories.

Daddy said that back during World War II when daylight savings time first began, the government said it would give workers one hour more of daylight. But the farmers in Scott and Wise Counties didn't like it because they said the extra hour of sunshine was drying out all their crops.

A man in Kentucky, Daddy continued without so much as pausing, made a list of all the men that he could whoop. He was showing the list around and bragging when one day a big fellow spoke up and said, "Hey, wait a minute, here. You've got my name on there and you can't whoop me." The first man looked at the big fellow and looked at his paper and replied, "Well then, I'll just scratch your name off my list."

Uncle Maynard said that a cousin of his went home drinking one night, back in his younger days, and it was pitch dark. As he approached the gate, he stuck his hands out to try to find it. But his hands and arms went between the gate's draw bars and he rammed his nose into one of the bars and the blood started flying. He went into the house and told his family, "Ain't it a shame when a man's nose is longer than his arms."

He said Delmer came in drinking one night and they heard him keep fumbling with something in the front room and ever so often he'd stomp and cuss. They went to see what he was doing and he was sitting in front of the sewing machine turning all the drawer knobs and cussing it because it wouldn't play music.

Then Uncle Maynard said that his great grandpa Robinette brought a drunk home with him at 2 a.m. one morning and woke up his wife and told her to fix him something to eat. She started cooking and grumbling. "What do you think I'm made of," she said, "iron?" The drunk heard her and raised up and said, "No, no, you're made out of the finest of steel or your tongue would've been worn out long ago."

Right after that incident, Uncle Maynard said, his great grandpa Robinette overheard his wife and a neighbor woman

120

talking. The other woman asked her why she got up all hours and fed her husband's friends—why she was so extra good to her husband all the time. "Great Grandma told the neighbor that she tried to be as good to her husband as she possibly could because she was afraid that down here in this life would be all the heaven he'd ever experience. Great Grandpa Robinette got to thinking about what she said, and from then on, went to church every Sunday and was as good a man as ever lived."

Daddy said that Uncle Marion Buchanan had a dog one time called old Drum that he said was the best minding dog he ever owned. "One day he was telling a bunch of us boys what a good dog that was and to prove it he ordered old Drum, who was curled up in front of the fireplace, to get out of the house. Well, Drum got up and headed for the bed, and quick as Uncle Marion saw what the dog was doing, he added, 'or under the bed one.' "

Uncle Victor said a man from Dry Fork owed a right big bill at the local store. One day he went to the owner and told him that he owed him right much and said, "I guess you've worried a right smart over it, haven't you?" The store owner answered that yes he had, actually. So the man said, "Well then, I don't see any use of both of us worrying, so I'll try not to let it bother me anymore."

Daddy said that was like the man who appeared before the judge in a divorce settlement. The judge told the man, "I'm awarding your ex-wife $200 per month."

"Well thank-you, judge," the man said, "and I'll try to chip in a little myself from time to time."

Then June Mead spoke up and said he had a neighbor once who decided he'd like to get him one of them divorces. So he went to the courthouse to see about it and they told him that to get a divorce, first of all, he'd have to file his subpoena. Well, he didn't like the sound of that at all, so he decided he didn't want a divorce as bad as he thought. He went back home and behaved himself from then on.

That was a type of grinning and snickering joke. No one actually laughed out loud, so they went on with their story telling.

Daddy started telling them again: "A man on Dry Fork said that when he was first married he loved his wife enough to eat her, and now he wished he had.

"And a Lawson man overheard two men arguing almost to the point of fighting, one day. He wanted to stop a fight, so he told them that it was okay for two people to see things different. He said, for instance, that if everyone saw everything just like him, every man would've wanted his wife. One of the men spoke up and said, yeah and if everyone had a been just like me, no one would've wanted her."

Uncle Victor said that, way back, that same Lawson man

ordered a clock from Sears and Roebuck. It was supposed to strike on the hour and half-hour. It did pretty good until in the middle of the night, sometime, it went haywire and struck 13 times. "Lordy mercy, wake up, honey," the man told his wife, "it's later than it's ever been."

Then Daddy started telling some jokes that he said people used to like to tell on the foreigners who came in there to build the railroad tracks and to work in the coal mines. "You all know about the Swede Tunnel down on Guest's River getting its name because so many Swedes were imported to work on it. Well, the foreigners, of course, spoke with an accent that the mountain people weren't used to hearing, so it sounded funny to the them.

"Anyway, back when Dr. Joe Wolfe was practicing in Coeburn, one of the German men's wife took sick. He took her to Doc Joe and after the doctor examined her, the man asked what was wrong with her. The doctor said he didn't know for sure, but before he could finish, the foreigner replied, 'I know you don't know doc, but what do you dank?'

"There also used to be a lot of Hungarians lived around here. And one of them lost his calf. You know they didn't have stock laws back then and everybody let their cows run out and had to hunt them up every evening. Well, he couldn't find his calf in all the usual places, so he put up some posters. The posters read, 'Me losey one bull calf. She havey three white feet, two more samey like. Anybody finey this calf, me pay everybody three dollars.'"

Grandma Hall spoke up and said that when her daddy worked in the mine and they lived in a mine shack, they had a lot of Hungarian neighbors. "Hunkies was what everyone called them. And they could bake the best bread of anybody in the camp. So people used to trade them parsnips, beans, tomatoes and potatoes for bread and it worked out good for everyone." Grandma said that she used to play with the Hungarian children and she taught them English and they taught her to count to ten in Hungarian. Then Grandma commenced: "one-re, you-re, ye-re, yea-re, yak-re, jim, jimark, jimack, jiminick, jifoop." I had heard Grandma relate that many times and always wondered if it really was Hungarian numbers that she was repeating.

Then Daddy said that back early in Wise County, parsnips was a staple food. "A lot of people would've starved to death had it not been for parsnips. One day a man was eating at a friend's house and they had parsnips for supper. Naturally he took out some, which he didn't care much for, and when he cleaned up his plate the neighbor's wife asked, 'like some parsnips?' meaning 'do you want some more.' Well, he thought she was asking if they were good, in other words was she a good cook, so he said 'yes' and she gave him some more. After the third or fourth helping of parsnips, he said, 'I like 'em all right, but don't give me no more.' "

Daddy said that Uncle Elbert Robinette, Mother's great uncle, and another man was pulling some logs with a team of oxen one day when they stalled. "Now Uncle Elbert was considered the strongest man that ever lived. So he decided that one of the ox wasn't pulling his share. Well, he took him out and got in the yoke beside the other ox. The ox outpulled him and almost broke his neck. So he yelled 'stop him, stop him.' But every time Uncle Elbert hollered, the other man whipped the ox and he went even faster. When they finally stopped, he asked the man why he kept whipping the ox. The man said, 'Oh, I thought you were saying 'pop him.' "

Then Daddy said that people used to live in cheap houses called boxed houses. "They were also built at sawmills and called sawmill shacks. The floor was straight from the sawmill, and the lumber was not planed. After the floor was laid, two boards were nailed together at a 90 degree angle and these were nailed at the four corners of the house. Two by fours or poles were nailed across the top of these and filled in between with boards (we called them planks). The boards didn't exactly fit together so it was stripped—thin, narrow lumber was nailed over the cracks. In many cases the roof only sloped one way and of course there was no ceiling. Well, I remember sleeping in my uncle's house and I could see the plank roof. I also could see the stars at night between the planks. Well one night it rained when I stayed there but the roof did not leak. It had been put together in such a way that the water ran right off the house."

After several questions about how houses used to be built, Daddy said that most people never actually locked their houses, but locks were put on the inside of the door and a slot was cut in the door so it could be unlocked from the outside. "Everyone who did lock their doors carried a door key, but everyone's keys, mostly skeleton keys, would open everyone else's doors."

Then Daddy said that when he was a boy, his dad liked his moleskin pants and his kangaroo shoes with the big ball toe. But younger men wore blue serge pants, he said.

Then Grandma Hall got to laughing and I knew she was remembering a funny story. So she said that when James (Daddy) was a boy, he always wanted some riding britches. So they saved milk and egg money until they could order him some. Finally, when the pants arrived, Daddy put them on and yelled, "now gitty up." When they didn't ride him anywhere, he got so upset, he cried.

Everybody looked at Daddy and laughed so Grandma told another one on him. She said that when Daddy was a little boy, everybody put a lot of patches on clothes because they couldn't afford to buy new. Grandma and Grandpa bragged on patches so Daddy would think they were something special. One time, however, they did order Daddy a new pair of pants. They had to go to Coeburn not long after that for supplies and told Daddy to put his new pants on. Well, he put them on and took the scissors and cut holes in the knees. "Lord, James, what have you done to your brand new pants," they said. "I want them Coeburn mans to know I have patches," he said with tears in his eyes.

Daddy said that people used to make money whatever way they could, and picking berries was one way to get some cash or barter for something they needed. "Berries brought ten cents a gallon, and that wasn't bad money. Most people didn't have a place to keep money because they didn't have furniture with drawers, except for their sewing machine. That's why everyone liked a sewing machine, because besides sewing with it, they could hide any money they might have, in the drawers. My aunt and her children went blackberry picking and the children were excited about getting some money for the sewing machine drawer. After they picked about all day, one of the little girls hollered from the far hillside to her mother, and told her how many berries she'd picked, and wanted to know how much money that would make them 'at home in the 'chine drawer, and all.' "

After that story, Labourn stood up, fiddled with the snap on the side of his overalls and said, "Well boys, let's all go on down to Possum Holler." Then he tilted his head back and shoved his chin out in a determined manner and headed out the door. Everybody began to put their bottles in the pop crates and saunter to the outside. I took my empty bottle with me because I wanted to keep it. Someday, I figured, I'd show it to my children and grandchildren while stirring their imaginations with stories of Possum Holler.

About 20 minutes after we got home we heard a pickup heading out the road like a hound after a fox. Daddy walked to the door—we left it standing open because the night was just beginning to pull back the heavy blanket of heat and let the trees fan the hollers. Daddy turned back from the door and said, "Hmmm, that looked like Victor's pickup."

The next morning Grandma Hall was hollering from the yard, "Ah James, ah James." When we went outside, she said that Labourn had died during the night. After he left the Top of the Hill, he went straight home, lay down on his bed and commenced to die. He called Victor's name, so Martha called to let him know that Labourn was asking for him. Victor sat by Labourn's bed all night. Labourn gave Victor his whittling knife, and then along after midnight sometime, Victor said, Labourn commenced to stare toward the far corner of the room. "Looky there, Vic, do you see it?" Labourn said.

"See what Labourn?"

"Heaven is coming for me. Can you see it?"

"I don't see it Labourn."

"Well, Vic," Labourn smiled, "it looks just like little Stoney Creek."

Then he closed his eyes and died. Labourn always thought Little Stoney Creek, which ran from above Bark Camp Lake down by hanging rock in Dungannon and into the Clinch River, was the prettiest place on the face of the earth.

That Sunday in church, we sang, "Where Could I go but to the Lord."[1]

> *Living below in this old sinful world*
> *Hardly a comfort can afford*
> *Striving along to face temptations sore*
> *Where could I go but to the Lord.*
>
> *chorus*
> *Where could I go, oh where could I go*
> *Seeking a refuge for my soul*
> *Needing a friend to help me in the end*
> *Where could I go but to the Lord.*

They said it was Labourn's favorite hymn.

Come spring, Mother and I started gathering our wild greens and herbs for eating and canning. We always had our first mess of fresh greens on Easter, so the gathering had become a sort of religious ritual for me. This time it was even more meaningful. I wanted to make sure I recognized and remembered everything—the medicinal plants and herbs especially. We gathered fewer of them each year and I was afraid I was forgetting. Yellowroot, bloodroot, burdock, catnip, mayapple, mustard, parsley, mint, wooly britches, ground cherries, milkweed, plantain, poke, pusley, camomile, red clover, violets, henband, rue, savory, Feverfew, Rat's Vein, rattlesnake king, beech bark, birch bark, slippery elm bark, Lobelia, ginseng, mullein, sassafras, golden seal, sheep sorrel, huckleberry leaves, fennel, balm of Gilead buds, several types of fern and a few others were about all I could remember. Mother's aunts, Grandpa Robinette's sisters—Aunt Nellie and Aunt Liz—were the only two midwives in the mountains for much of the early 1900's and their sister Aunt Mary was one of the best herb doctors in the area. Mother said they used to gather hundreds of plants for their medicines. Mother had already forgotten a lot of the plants they used for curing people.

I believed the mountains were gradually withdrawing the life-giving information they had once so willingly shared. They no longer trusted us. Or, perhaps, the mountains were still willing to whisper their secrets but we no longer took the time to listen.

Anyway, that Easter, we sat down to a dinner of, among other things, newly gathered field greens, which reminded us of the newness of life in Christ. And since Easter greens consisted of the bitter herbs of the field spoken of in the Bible, it also reminded us of the "bitter cup" which Christ willingly drank for us. The whole Easter ritual, from the gathering to the dinner itself, was a vital part of my spiritual constancy.

CHAPTER 16

ONE DYING, ONE LEAVING

Twelfth grade wasn't much different from the other grades, except it was moving faster. There was always something to do to get ready for graduation. One morning, during homeroom, we selected our senior class song. We picked "Look Down, Look Down that Lonesome Road Before You Travel on," for our song. I looked, but I couldn't see very far down my lonesome road, and, of course, I had no choice but to travel. But I wasn't sure where this path would lead me. I yearned for familiar paths. So, that night, I looked into my pool, and there were the faces of all those who had gone before. And for the first time, they responded. Grandpa Robinette was among them now and he was pointing to a map. He traced a path from France to Ireland to America. Move on, Geraldine, they said smiling, it's time now. But what about everyone else, what about Pansy, I asked. They were silent.

Graduations are like the color purple—royal, pompous affairs with a touch of merriment. But they harbor too much blue for real revelry. We were a sea of black and white canaries prancing and bobbing before proud and anxious lip-biting parents. Speeches that were much too long included words such as achieve, vision, heights, accomplish, purpose, resolve, and cognizance. Finally, the tassle ceremony signified that we had achieved a certain goal and we could attain new heights of knowledge that would surely lead to truth, wisdom, and success. By the time the whole thing was over, they had spouted a chain of grandiloquent terms so long that it actually could have hitched our wagons to the stars—which was something else we were encouraged to do.

Unbeknownst to me, Mother and Daddy had been setting aside money for my graduation for years. And graduation morning, Daddy came driving an almost new Plymouth car to the house and handed me the keys. It was as black and beautiful as moonless nights. Rodney and I rode together in my new car to graduation and after the ceremony, we hopped into it and drove downtown to the Creamy Dreamy to celebrate. The Creamy Dreamy made absolutely the best milkshakes in the world. We ordered hotdogs with real homemade chile and milkshakes and sat down in a booth in the back, to be alone. Rodney had been wanting to "set the date" for a long time but I had been dragging my feet, even though I knew in my heart that marrying him was the thing to do. Rodney was a good christian, highly intelligent, and kind-hearted—three characteristics I prized above all else. I loved his big brown sad-looking eyes, and I loved him.

He had caught me unawares and slipped right inside my heart. Mother and Daddy really wanted me to go to college and I wanted to get my degree someday. But it seemed like it would be better if I worked while Rodney got his degree and then I could get mine without much of a financial problem. I wanted Mother to go to nursing school and I knew she would put if off if she could get me to go to college. Of course, I'd finally saved up enough money to buy her a ring and if Rodney and I got married, I'd have to use the money for us. And an education would probably mean we'd never come back to the mountains to live. Rodney and I talked over all of these heartbreaking choices as the jukebox played "Wonderland by Night" and we slurped the last bubbles from the bottom of our milkshakes. Rodney usually got strawberry and I always got chocolate. As we started to leave, I bought a chocolate milkshake to go, for Pansy.

Pansy didn't get to attend my graduation because she hadn't been feeling well for several days. She had been chilling and had lost her appetite. A lot people in the area had gotten the flue and Pansy's mother thought that might be what Pansy had. Still, she tried to fetch the nurse who lived in Crab Orchard. She always made house calls and gave people shots of penicillin when they took sick. But when Pansy's mother went for her she was visiting her daughter in Florida. Anyway, I thought Pansy would enjoy the milkshake and I'd never known her to turn down chocolate.

Rodney and I decided to go by my house first to let Mother and Daddy know we'd gotten back from town with the car still in one piece. As we rounded the bend past Grandma Hall's house, I noticed that the Jeep was parked in front of the house, but the car was gone. Daddy met us on the porch. Pansy had gotten worse, he said, and as soon as he and Mother got home from graduation, Pansy's mother told them Pansy was burning up with a fever and she needed a ride to St. Mary's. Daddy had no more than gotten the words out of his mouth until Rodney and I jumped back into my little black Plymouth and headed to St. Mary's hospital in Norton. During the trip to the hospital I was in some kind of dream-state. Nothing looked the right color. Trees and mountains were a gray-green and I couldn't tell where the gray was coming from. Sunlight slanted sideways and colors and shadows retreated when I tried to focus. Rodney drove the car, but when he talked, his voice came from a long way off, as though he wasn't sitting beside me in the car at all. And it seemed like we kept going faster then slower, now crawling, now airborn. When we parked at St. Mary's, I was holding my scarf in my hand and had tied several knots in it. I didn't remember taking it from around my neck. Immediately I was inside and I kept telling the lady at the front desk I was there to see Pansy McCarty, and she kept looking for her name. Then I saw Mother and Mrs. McCarty come around the corner from the right. Mrs.

McCarty's head was drooped over to the side as though her neck was broken and Mother was holding her up as they tried to walk down the hall. Tears were rolling down mother's face and dropping from her chin onto her dress, and I could hear Mrs. McCarty sobbing, "My baby, my baby." I opened my mouth to scream or something then I felt my knees buckle like the blade on a pocket knife, and everything went dark.

When I came to, I was still in the hospital and a nurse was holding something in front of my nose that had the kick of a mule. They said it was smelling salts. When Mother saw I was allright, she started on home with Mrs. McCarty because a doctor had given her a sedative and said she needed to go to bed. As he helped me to the car, Rodney said Pansy had pneumonia, but I didn't believe people still died from pneumonia.

"But Pansy wasn't like regular people," he said. "She was more fragile."

"Fragile, like the butterflies she loved so much," I said. But I didn't want to talk about it anymore, because I just couldn't reconcile it in my mind. When we got into the car, I put my feet on the car seat, wrapped my arms around my legs, and propped my chin on my knees. Then we rode home in silence. It occurred to me on the way home that I should have asked to see Pansy before they took her away and turned her to stone with their cadaverous marinade. There was something I'd like to have told her.

Rodney stayed at my house all evening. We sat together on the porch swing and watched the many shades of evening. Some lilacs and mint had grabbed the evening air and drifted around the holler bringing calm to the night. Still, neither of us ate supper. Mother took a big pot of chicken and dumplings, a bowl of cooked salad peas, and a pineapple chiffon cake over to the McCarty's house. When she got back home, she said Pansy's grandmother was holding up pretty good but Pansy's mother was in bad shape. About midnight, Rodney walked on home, but I sat in the porch swing all night. Mother never asked me to come inside, she just brought a quilt and put over me because it was getting a little cool. Along about daylight, I got some paper and jotted down my jagged thoughts. It seemed like the right thing to do.

Pansy's funeral was held in the church house at the Top of the Hill. There were so many people and flowers, some of both had to wait outside during the service. They had placed my flowers behind Pansy's casket and I was glad they did. It was made to look like the portals of glory with a butterfly just about to go inside. The florist usually put a dove perched and ready to go into heaven but I insisted they substitute a butterfly and they did. Of course, they looked me up and down when I asked for the butterfly like they thought I was with some strange religion or something. But I knew that like the butterflies she wrote about, Pansy rode warm winds to heaven. A group from Dry Fork called the Jubilaires sang because Mother and Daddy didn't think they could hold up. They sang "Gathering Buds for the Master's Bouquet," and "Death is only a Dream." Then Preacher Ruff commenced to preach his funeral sermon about the pure river of water of life, clear as a crystal, proceeding out of the throne of God and of the Lamb, and how that in that city, God shall wipe away all tears and there shall be no more death or sorrow or crying or pain. Then he told about the gates of pearl and streets of gold as pure as transparent glass and how there would be no need for the sun because the Lamb of God is the light and the Glory of God would light it. Then he said the saved would walk in that beautiful place. He didn't say they'd be there, he said they'd "walk" there. And when he said walk, it occurred to me that for the first time Pansy was walking. And the first streets her little feet touched were pure gold. And I knew that she not only walked down those streets, she ran. And she ran like the wind, and when Jesus looked at her and smiled, she placed her finger to her temple and said, "It seemed like the right thing to do."

Just as I was seeing Pansy running and laughing, I felt something wet on my hands which I had cupped in my lap. I looked down and realized it was my own tears, flowing from my eyes like a river, and filling my hands. Finally, we filed by the casket, isle by isle, as the quartet sang, "Savior Gently Take Me Home."

We followed Pansy to the Bond graveyard above my house and said our final farewells. Then we gathered around the grave, the men removed their hats, and sang "Jesus Loves Me":

> Jesus loves me this I know
> For the Bible tells me so
> Little ones to him belong
> They are weak, but He is strong.

Pansy had a church song book with hundreds of hymns, but Jesus Loves Me was still her favorite.

After the service, Mother told me that Mrs. McCarty wanted me to come over to their house, she had something for me. I took my time getting there, stopping at the spring a while and then waiting for the wind in the oak grove. When I finally reached the door, people were coming and going, bring more food. Mrs. McCarty thrust a box of Pansy's most beloved books at me and then she turned and ran into the back room, holding a handkerchief to her face. I stood there a minute, startled, then I gathered it all up and walked away, bearing the vapor of Pansy's presence in my arms.

The next Saturday, I decided to look at the books and put them away for safe keeping. On the very top was the book of poems by Emily Dickinson that I had gotten Pansy for Christmas many years ago. Inside the book was the blue ribbon I'd given her when I won my first foot race at the Possum Holler fair. Pansy had sewn the ribbon to cardboard and used if for a bookmark. That way, it was always in front of her as a reminder. I took out the bookmark and read where Pansy had been reading.

Adrift! A little boat adrift!
And night is coming down!
Will no one guide a little boat
Unto the nearest town?

So sailors say, on yesterday,
Just as the dusk was brown,
One little boat gave up its strife,
And gurgled down and down.

But angels say, on yesterday,
Just as the dawn was red,
One little boat o'erspent with gales
Retrimmed its masts, redecked its sails
Exultant, onward sped![1]

After weeks of going over and over our choices, Rodney and I decided it was time to move on with our lives. He didn't want a big wedding. I wanted to get married in the churchhouse at the Top of the Hill, but I didn't see where it really mattered, so we asked Preacher Ruff to marry us down at the manse the last of August. Mother took me to Norton and picked out the prettiest white tafeta dress I'd ever seen in my life. It had a little lace see-through jacket that was covered with tiny bows, love knots the sales lady called them, with a miniature pearl in the center of each one. It was tea length. I'd never heard of that before. But I hated for Mother to spend that kind of money on a dress for me when the dresses she wore were all homemade. Of course, Mother could make dresses that were prettier than store bought. She borrowed Grandma's catalogues and made my clothes and her clothes by looking at the pictures.

Rodney and I read that the University of Virginia had married student housing at Copeley Hill. They had small houses and a trailer park. I called and talked to them and they said they

1. <u>Bloomsbury Poetry Classics: Selected Poems of Emily Dickinson</u>, "Adrift! A Little Boat Adrift!" Copyright (c) 1993 by Bloomsbury Publishing Ltd., St. Martin's Press, Inc., New York, NY.

had some empty trailer spaces and they could reserve one for us. So we decided the most economical thing to do would be buy a trailer, since they came furnished. We took the money I'd saved for Mother's ring, went to a trailer lot in Johnson City, and paid down on a new 10 X 42 trailer. They were going to deliver it free of charge for us to Copeley Hill Trailer Park in Charlottesville. It would be there when we got there. So we planned the wedding for 10 a.m., allowing us time to make Charlottesville by nightfall.

Rodney took the money he'd saved and bought me a set of rings, Wedding Bells. He had been told that he'd better take a bell to the wedding because it would be the only thing there with a ring. He couldn't let that happen.

I called the personnel department at UVa and asked about a job, and although they didn't have any openings there, they said the local telephone company was hiring. I called them and got the promise of a job as soon as I arrived. I'd be making $42.50 a week without overtime. I knew we wouldn't have any trouble financially because if it was one thing I'd learned from Mother, it was how to manage money.

We didn't send out invitations to our wedding. We just invited family. Lucy and Shirley came too because they would be graduating next year and leaving the mountains for good. We didn't know if we'd ever see each other again. And Diana drove down and brought me a blue garter to wear. She made sure I had something old, new, borrowed and blue. She fussed over me like a mother hen. Before the ceremony began, I heard Rodney's Aunt Frances Clay ask Mother wasn't it going to be hard for her to give me up. But Mother said that she was reading in the Bible the other night that "the earth is the Lord's and all they that dwell therein," so she knew the Lord would continue to care for me. "And anyway," she said, "I'm glad to see her marry such a good boy."

Mrs. Ruff, the preacher's wife, decorated the living room of the manse with fresh-cut flowers and candles and we said our vows before God and family including my younger cousins who found something squeaky in the room and squeaked and giggled all through the ceremony. It actually made it a very pleasant wedding and I wouldn't have had it any other way.

Mother gave me half or more of everything she owned. And we had my little Plymouth loaded down with sheets, quilts, towels, and all kinds of kitchen utensils. After the wedding, we changed clothes, I hugged everyone and cried, then we headed up the road for Charlottesville and the beginning of a new life together. I waved at all of them, and kept waving, until the road ate up the sky.

I was leaving some mighty important things unattended to in the mountains. But I knew I would correct them one day. I would get Mother that ring with the gracefully twining garland of white gold orange blossoms, and I would get Pansy a headstone with butterflies carved on it. The McCarty's couldn't afford to mark her grave.

As we neared Abingdon, I looked back toward home. The mountains were fading behind me like a rose closing for the night, petal by petal. Good-bye sweet mountains, I whispered and faced straight ahead—leaning into the wind. Rodney squeezed my hand. "Farther on, still go forward, count the milestones one by one," he began to sing. Then I joined him, in pure harmony, "Jesus will forsake you never. It gets better farther on."

Photo by Joe Tennis, *Bristol Herald Courier*

About the Author

The author, D. Geraldine Lawson, is a native of Coeburn (Possum Holler) in Wise County, Virginia, with family roots in the Appalachian Mountains as deep and enduring as the ancient oaks that inhabit the hills and hollers. Geraldine attended Clinch Valley College in Wise and graduated with a bachelor's degree in English from Hollins College near Roanoke. She is working on her master's degree. She has taught school and worked as writer/public relations specialist for Virginia Tech in Blacksburg where many of her articles appeared in national and international newspapers and magazines.

Geraldine is president and executive director of Attic Productions, Inc., a community theater group in Botetourt County. She writes plays, short stories, poetry, and is working with her Dad on a second book.

Her husband, Rod Lawson, also a native of Wise County, attended two years at Clinch Valley College and earned his bachelor's and master's degrees in electrical engineering from the University of Virginia. He is an electrical engineer with General Electric in Salem. They reside in Fincastle. They have three children: Dr. David Lawson, Dr. Lianna Lawson, and John Lawson who is working toward his master's degree in philosophy.

Photo by J. O. T. and a Stewart and a Camera

About the Author

The author, Jo Costain (J. T. awich), is a native of Coeburn (Fostume Holler), in Wise County, Virginia, with deeply rooted in the Appalachian Mountains as deep and enduring as the ancient oak that is both the Birch and Holler. Co-graduated Clinch Valley College in Wise and graduated with a bachelor's degree in English Language/Composition Romance. She is working on her master's degree. She has taught school and worked as writer/public relations specialist for Virginia Tech in Blacksburg, where many of her articles appeared in national and international newspaper and magazines.

Her native is president and executive director of Wise Adjustment, Inc. an community leadership group in Dickenson County. She writes plays, short stories, poetry and is working with her Dan on a second novel.

Her husband, Rod, is a native of Scott County, attended three years at the High Valley College and carried his bachelors and master's degree in electrical engineering from the University of Virginia. He is an electrical engineer with General Electric in Salem, consulting in Lincoln site. They have three children: Brad, David, Twain, Deja and John Lawson who is working toward his master's degree in philosophy.